P9-BVH-295

Advance praise for *Jesus the Evangelist*

Jesus the Evangelist: A Gospel Guide to the New Evangelization invites Catholics to read the Gospels through the lens of the New Evangelization and rediscover the tradition of Catholic evangelization. Allan F. Wright has provided a valuable tool for parish evangelization teams, hospitality ministries, and adult formation groups interested in actively participating in the Church's mission to call all people to an encounter with the Living Christ.

> His Eminence, Cardinal Donald Wuerl
> Archbishop of Washington, D.C.

Allan Wright makes the events and people of the New Testament come alive for his readers in a lively and engaging style. With keen insight, he draws us into the New Evangelization, not as a program, but as the very mission of the Church in our day.

> Most Reverend Arthur Serratelli
> Bishop of Paterson, New Jersey

When Catholics hear the call to a New Evangelization, they often wonder how to go about it. Allan F. Wright shows us how, in very clear and biblical terms, drawing from the original and inspired evangelizers: Matthew, Mark, Luke, and John. Readable and practical, this is a book that will really empower Catholic laypeople and Catholic parishes to move, as Allan puts it, from maintenance mode to mission.

> Scott Hahn, author of
> *A Father Who Keeps His Promises*

Jesus
the Evangelist

*A Gospel Guide
to the New Evangelization*

ALLAN F. WRIGHT

Franciscan
MEDIA
Cincinnati, Ohio

Scripture passages have been taken from *New Revised Standard Version Bible,* copyright ©1989 by the Division of Christian Education of the National Council of the Churches of Christ in the U.S.A., and used by permission. All rights reserved.

Cover design by Candle Light Studios
Cover image © Studio-Annika
Book design by Mark Sullivan

LIBRARY OF CONGRESS CATALOGING-IN-PUBLICATION DATA
Wright, Allan F., 1964-
Jesus the evangelist : a gospel guide to the new evangelization / Allan F. Wright.
pages cm
Includes bibliographical references and index.
ISBN 978-1-61636-542-4 (alk. paper)
1. Jesus Christ—Evangelistic methods. 2. Evangelistic work—Biblical teaching. 3. Bible. N.T. Gospels—Criticism, interpretation, etc. I. Title.
BT590.E8W75 2013
266'.2—dc23
2012048303
ISBN 978-1-61636-542-4

Copyright ©2013, Allan Wright. All rights reserved.

Published by Franciscan Media
28 W. Liberty St.
Cincinnati, OH 45202
www.FranciscanMedia.org

Printed in the United States of America.
Printed on acid-free paper.
13 14 15 16 17   5 4 3 2 1

To my wife Desiree
and our three beautiful little girls:
Sophia, Cataleen, and Abigail
Joy upon joy upon joy!

Lauder Deo Mariaeque

CONTENTS

ACKNOWLEDGMENTS   *ix*

PREFACE   *xi*

PART ONE
  Chapter One
    The Church's Essential Mission of Evangelization   *1*

PART TWO: THE WITNESS OF ST. JOHN THE EVANGELIST
  Chapter Two
    John 1:14 | *The Word Became Flesh and Lived Among Us*   *11*
  Chapter Three
    John 3 | *Nicodemus: Evangelization and Confrontation*   *17*
  Chapter Four
    John 4:7 | *Evangelizing the Marginalized and Outcast*   *24*
  Chapter Five
    John 5:1–9 | *Evangelization One Person at a Time*   *31*
  Chapter Six
    John 7:53—8:11 | *In Mercy and Truth*   *37*
  Chapter Seven
    John 11:38–44 | *Power to Bring New Life*   *42*

PART THREE: THE WITNESS OF ST. LUKE THE EVANGELIST
  Chapter Eight
    Luke 5:27–32 | *Calling Others for Discipleship*   *49*
  Chapter Nine
    Luke 6:46–49 | *A Solid Foundation*   *55*
  Chapter Ten
    Luke 8:4–8 | *Sowing Seeds, Preparing Soil*   *62*
  Chapter Eleven
    Luke 10:25–37 | *Social Justice as Evangelization*   *68*

Chapter Twelve
Luke 15:1–7 | *The Seeking Shepherd: The Model for Evangelization* 75
Chapter Thirteen
Luke 22:39–46 | *Prayer: Strength for the Evangelist* 81
Chapter Fourteen
Luke 24:27–32 | *The Eucharist: The Heart of Evangelization* 86

PART FOUR: THE WITNESS OF ST. MARK THE EVANGELIST
Chapter Fifteen
Mark 1:16–20 | *Engaging People Where They Are* 93
Chapter Sixteen
Mark 2:1–12 | *Developing a Missionary Mind-Set* 98
Chapter Seventeen
Mark 5:30–31 | *Evangelization on the Way* 103
Chapter Eighteen
Mark 12:29–34 | *Apologetics: Scripture and Catechesis in Evangelization* 109

PART FIVE: THE WITNESS OF ST. MATTHEW THE EVANGELIST
Chapter Nineteen
Matthew 9:35–38 | *Motivated by Compassion* 119
Chapter Twenty
Matthew 10:5–10 | *The "Little" Commission* 126
Chapter Twenty-One
Matthew 11:28–30 | *The Invitation of Jesus the Evangelist* 134
Chapter Twenty-Two
Matthew 28:16–20 | *The Great Commission* 140

PART SIX: MOVING THE CHURCH FROM A MAINTENANCE MIND-SET TO ONE OF MISSION 147

NOTES 159

ACKNOWLEDGMENTS

I'd like to thank my wife, Desiree, and our children: Sophia, Cataleen, and Abigail, who are a continual source of joy, strength, and support in my life. They are a reminder that being a man of the family is the best way to serve the Church.

For my mother, Jane Wright, my first and best teacher of the faith who is a constant source of joy and hope. For my Dad, Ivan F. Wright, whose memory, humor, and love is never far from me.

In grateful appreciation of the Most Reverend Arthur J. Serratelli, S.T.D., S.S.L., D.D., Bishop of Paterson, New Jersey, a man who lives his life from the Eucharist.

To the Missionaries of Charity Sisters (Contemplative) and to all the M.C. Sisters in formation in Plainfield, New Jersey, past and present, who are a weekly reminder of God's love, peace, and joy. You give me great hope for the future of the Church and for the world. You make me a better disciple of Jesus.

To my friends who give life, form and expression to the New Evangelization at St. Paul Inside the Walls, The Catholic Center for Evangelization at Bayley-Ellard in Madison, New Jersey.

In grateful appreciation to Amber Dolle and her family for her willingness and time to look things over for me and to provide guidance along the way lest my sentences go on and on and on...

To Mary Carol Kendzia, for her assistance and care in seeing this project through and to all who work at Franciscan Media.

Fortiter in re, suaviter in modo

It's an exciting time to be Catholic. The enthusiasm of the first disciples continues to be our own as we carry on the mission of Jesus in our day. The Holy Spirit came down on the first believers, people just like us with fears and anxieties, and made them evangelizers. That Spirit is being poured out on us today. In response to that Spirit, the Catholic Church is moving in a direction to utilize all her resources and energies in the essential mission of the Church that is evangelization.

In facing the challenges that lie ahead we need to pray, to listen, to dialogue, and to articulate the person of Jesus Christ to others in a way that resonates with the human condition, with the human heart and mind. We do it not because of dwindling statistics but because Jesus commands us to do so. While there is no perfect program, there is a perfect person: Jesus Christ, who is our model in all things. In conforming our lives to his and by being animated by the Holy Spirit, we can evangelize like he evangelized in word, deed, and in power.

It is my hope that this book will assist those who read it to develop the mind of Christ and an evangelizing mind-set so that we may bear fruit that will last. In studying the life of Christ we observe how he reached out to those who were religious, to those who doubted, and to those who were on the margins of society. The models for parishes, individuals, and ecclesial movements will differ according to the various situations they face, yet the model remains the same: Jesus Christ.

Allan F. Wright

Feast of St. Thérèse of Lisieux of the Child Jesus,

"The Little Flower," Patroness of Missions

PART ONE

CHAPTER ONE

The Church's Essential Mission of Evangelization

Ten years after the close of the Second Vatican Council and one year after the 1974 synod of bishops, Pope Paul VI issued an apostolic exhortation entitled *Evangelii Nuntiandi.* In this document, the pontiff stated that the Church "exists in order to evangelize, that is to say, in order to preach and teach, to be the channel of the gift of grace, to reconcile sinners with God, and to perpetuate Christ's sacrifice in the Mass, which is the memorial of His death and glorious resurrection."[1] Blessed John Paul II recognized that efforts to reawaken the faith in traditionally Christian parts of the world were imperative, and he articulated this in an address to the Latin American bishops in 1983. This term—New Evangelization—would be used for the mission of the entire Church to rekindle the faith in those already baptized but who have fallen away from Christ and his Church.

The phrase, "The Church exists in order to evangelize" may be both confusing and surprising to Catholics in the pew. It is confusing because many Catholics don't know what the word *evangelize* means, and surprising because many people think that the Catholic Church exists primarily to provide aid to those in need. While the Catholic

Church does spend much of her time and resources coordinating relief services for a multitude of social ills, the call to evangelization comes to us from Christ. It is a movement of the Holy Spirit who stands by our side since the beginning reminding us of this essential mission.

Simply put, evangelization is proclaiming the good news of Jesus Christ to every person and in every situation. The original language of the New Testament, Koine Greek, gives us the word εὐαγγέλιον, which we translate as "good news." In Latin the word is translated as *evangelium*. In Greek, this word is used when someone is making an announcement. It has no religious meaning in and of itself, but Christians took hold of it when announcing the "good news" of Jesus's death and resurrection. Catholic evangelization proposes not only the message of Jesus Christ, but the person of Jesus Christ. The person and the message are inseparable.

For many Catholics, the word *evangelization* might sound too "Protestant." We may have in our mind the image of the television evangelist who tells us what we must believe or face damnation. Catholics have a history of keeping their faith to themselves. The discrimination that plagued an untold number of Catholic immigrants in the United States created a culture where faith was a private matter. It wasn't always popular or easy to be a Catholic, and Catholics had to quietly live out their faith in the midst of discrimination. This understated, quiet witness of faith is, of course, a form of evangelization, but it established the notion that sharing the faith was not necessary. This continues to affect the mind-set of today's Catholic.

Times have changed, however. Rather than flee from the word *evangelization*, we should embrace the opportunity to rediscover the beautiful tradition and practice of Catholic evangelization found throughout the two-thousand-year history of the Church, rooted in Scripture and Tradition.

The most explicit explanation of the New Evangelization is found in Pope John Paul II's encyclical *Redemptoris Missio*. In this letter, the Holy Father describes three different situations that are ripe for evangelization: *mission ad gentes*, Christian communities, and the New Evangelization. *Ad Gentes* is Latin for "to the nations." This describes a situation where Christ and his Gospel are not known. "Christian communities" speaks to communities in the Church that "carry out her activity and pastoral care." This is the ongoing evangelization of those who are active and are fervent in the faith. "The New Evangelization" describes a situation between the first two, "where entire groups of the baptized have lost a living sense of the faith, or even no longer consider themselves members of the Church, and live a life far removed from Christ and his Gospel. In this case what is needed is a 'new evangelization' or a 're-evangelization.'"[2]

In this present age, the Catholic Church is calling us to evangelize as Jesus did, in word and deed, to reach out to those who have been baptized but have left the Church. Our voices must be heard with renewed joy and vigor in proclaiming Jesus Christ. What we are proposing is not simply the fact of the resurrection of Jesus, but the life-transforming power that Christ's resurrection brings in each of our own lives. Proper evangelization makes others aware that they have value in God's eyes, that they are loved, and that God desires an intimate relationship with them through Jesus Christ. We invite them into this relationship. Our words about Jesus and the way we live should bear witness to this ongoing transformation in our own lives.

St. Peter wrote, "Always be ready to make your defense to anyone who demands from you an accounting for the hope that is in you" (1 Peter 3:15). St. Paul, in writing to the community in Rome, asks, "And how are they to believe in one of whom they have never heard? And how are they to hear without someone to proclaim him?" (Romans 10:14) Pope John Paul II declared, "No believer in Christ, no institution of the Church can avoid this supreme duty: to proclaim Christ to all peoples."[3] The message is clear that preaching and proclaiming Christ has been the consistent call of the Church since Pentecost. Evangelization is not about expounding the details of doctrine, apologetics, or about proving others wrong; evangelization is about the proclamation of a person, Jesus Christ.

How do we speak of Jesus? When should we do it? How do we articulate our faith in a meaningful way to a suspicious and secularized culture or to those who no longer have faith? How can we communicate the good news to people who know nothing of God and expect nothing from God? The challenge is not new. Jesus faced the same problem, as did St. Paul. Many missionaries and evangelists down through the centuries had the same task with various degrees of success and failures. We should learn from their experiences in our efforts to present the good news of Jesus in this present age.

We need to focus on Jesus, the master evangelist, as our starting point in evangelization. By studying the life of the greatest evangelist of all time, we can truly model Christ. He listened, observed, and spoke to people—religious or not—about the greatest news ever: God's personal love for each one of us. When we take the time to do this, "Church" will not be an activity that we are involved in, or a place where we go, but rather it will be who we are as Christians.

The responsibility of spreading the message of Jesus will not be for a select few in the Church, but will overflow from who we are in Christ. It is then that we can be the Church Pope Benedict XVI calls for as he spoke to students of the Roman Pontifical Universities in St. Peter's Square in October 2007: "The Church's evangelizing mission requires not only that the Gospel message be spread everywhere, *but that it penetrate deeply into the way people think, into their criteria for making judgments and their behavior.* In a word, the entire culture of modern man must be permeated by the Gospel."[4]

Why the Need for a New Evangelization?

The New Evangelization is aimed at a specific group of people: fallen-away or lapsed Catholics, and those baptized Catholics who don't consider God or religion important in their lives. Most Catholics recognize the need for this type of evangelization. After all, most people know someone who is a baptized Catholic but no longer practices the faith. John Paul II wanted the faithful to clearly recognize this reality, and it has become the task of individual communities to reach out in new and innovative ways to these groups.

Catholics make up the largest religious group in the United States, encompassing approximately one quarter of all Americans. The CARA Report, (Center for Applied Research in the Apostolate, Georgetown University) states that there are currently 22.5 million people who were "baptized and raised Catholic who no longer self-identify as Catholic." There are 16.2 million people who identify as Catholic but who are not in a household registered with a parish (although technically there is no requirement to register). Finally, there are some "23.8 million self-identified Catholics (many not registered with a parish) who do *not* attend Mass even at Christmas or Easter."[5] These statistics should move us to tears.

What an astounding number of people who say they are Catholic but don't even bother to go to Mass! What does that reveal about Catholic identity and what it means to belong to the Catholic Church for so many? How was the Catholic faith modeled in their childhood home? The truth is there is much work to be done.

We realize that there are those who will not believe for any number of reasons. Jesus himself, the master evangelist, experienced this rejection at the end of the Bread of Life discourse, as it is recorded in John 6:66: "Because of this many of his disciples turned back and no longer went about with him." The apostles were convinced that Jesus had the words of eternal life. They did not completely understand everything Jesus said and did, yet in faith they followed—as do we, for we have experienced the love of Christ.

There are some who will never follow Christ because his teaching is too difficult. Others find it easier to live day to day rather than explore the possibility that there is a God. For these, the philosophical explanations and arguments are too time-consuming. Like the twelve, we know that the one we follow has the words of eternal life. He has revealed himself to us and his love continues to transform us.

The Necessity of a Biblical, Christ-Centered Foundation

So how do we evangelize? The expressions of evangelization are many which will be discussed in the chapters of this book. Most importantly, if the Church is to make a significant inroads with its evangelizing efforts, it is essential that we learn from Jesus. In studying Jesus in the Gospels we learn from the master.

Christ comes intimately to us in his living word, the Bible. The gift of sacred Scripture is for all. St. Jerome is famously quoted as having said, "Ignorance of the Scriptures is ignorance of Christ."[6] Yet, I have heard many Catholics say they were told not to read the Bible.

The Catholic Church encourages the study of Scripture and has provided many tools to aid us in this endeavor. Documents such as *Dei Verbum*, *Divino Afflante Spiritu*, and *Providentissimus Deus* all encourage Scripture reading by the faithful. The *Catechism of the Catholic Church* has a beautiful section, (*CCC*, 101–141), that speaks of the inspiration in and truth of the Bible. One of the most compelling statements in this section asserts, "The Church 'forcefully and specifically exhorts all the Christian faithful...to learn "the surpassing knowledge of Jesus Christ," by frequent reading of the divine Scriptures'" (*CCC*, 133).[7]

It is vital to return to the knowledge and charism of our founder, Jesus Christ, to study the way he evangelized. St. Catherine of Siena said, "Love follows knowledge."[8] When we know Christ, read Scripture prayerfully, and contemplate his word, our love for him will increase. When we allow Christ into our hearts and minds through the study of his word, then his thirst for souls will become our thirst. His joy becomes our joy. His hope becomes our hope. The two become one.

No Condemnation for the "Old Evangelization"

The call for a New Evangelization is not a condemnation of past efforts by the Church and her members. While there have been parents, parishes, and catechists who, for perhaps many reasons, have failed to pass on the authentic faith of the Church as handed down by the apostles, the New Evangelization is not a direct response to any such failures.

The Church must continually evaluate the changing society and culture. We realize that we need new ways of engaging a secular culture that no longer views God as relevant. The majority of our young adults have no ties to a local parish. The sense of religious obligation, which was instilled in Catholics in past generations, is simply no longer a reality. Rather than bemoan and lament days gone by, the Catholic Church is calling us to engage a fallen world as Jesus did.

As in a sporting event or a military operation, evangelizers have to strategize and act in a manner corresponding to what is happening on the field. When a battle plan is adapted or a team changes its tactics mid-game, it is not an acknowledgment of failure. It is not to suggest that the soldiers who already fought were inadequate or that the players were incompetent. Strategy always needs to take into account new circumstances and adjust accordingly. Old ways of being Church must give life to new expressions of who we are as Church.

Converting the "Militant" Catholic Mind-Set to an Evangelizing Mind-Set

In the Catholic Church we have the Church militant, which struggles against sin and the devil, and the Church triumphant, which comprises our brothers and sisters in heaven. The Church militant has an ardent faith in Jesus and a committed spiritual life. It prays the rosary and the chaplet of divine mercy, attends Eucharistic Adoration, participates in prayer groups and so on. While so many have lapsed in faith, it remains faithful.

In my experience with the New Evangelization however, I have found that often times those who are most faithful to the traditions of the Church are least compassionate to those who no longer practice the faith. There can be a disconnect in what they see as adherence to Church teaching and the call of Christ to reach out to others in a way that is welcoming and inviting.

There is a tendency to adopt an us-against-them mind-set toward the world, or toward struggling and lapsed Catholics. They can become self-righteous and condescending toward those who no longer go to Church or who question belief in God. I have met people who will fly to visit a religious shrine halfway around the world, yet they fail to speak to a neighbor across the street who no longer goes to church. Some will travel thousands of miles to view an apparition in a field, yet they fail to invite someone to the greatest miracle ever, the Eucharist.

In order for the New Evangelization to flourish, we need the faith of "militant" Catholics. We need their knowledge of the traditions of the Church, their determination and perseverance, and their devotion to our Blessed Mother. However, we also need them to be open to the Holy Spirit so that God can stir their hearts and allow them to articulate the faith to others in a way that is joyful and inviting.

As Archbishop Rino Fisichella, president of the Pontifical Council for Promoting the New Evangelization, recently stated during an address on Vatican Radio, that we need evangelizers "who have a profound sense of belonging to the Church and the Christian community but at the same time who are open to others. And also a good dose of joy and enthusiasm, which is never a bad thing!"[9]

CHAPTER TWO

JOHN 1:14

The Word Became Flesh and Lived Among Us

. . .

And the Word became flesh and lived among us, and we have seen his glory, the glory as of a father's only son, full of grace and truth.

. . .

"In the beginning…" So begins the prologue of St. John's Gospel as it references God's act of creation in the book of Genesis. The crescendo of this poetic masterpiece arrives in verse 14: "And the Word became flesh and lived among us." In the original Greek, the word we translate as "lived" is best translated as "tabernacled." It may sound strange to our ears—"Tabernacled among us"—but it was chosen by John to link God's coming in the flesh in the person of Jesus Christ to the Exodus event where a tabernacle was constructed for the dwelling of the Lord God. Such is the desire of God to be with his people.

God had indeed dwelt among his people. In the book of Genesis we read that God was walking in the cool of the day searching for Adam and Eve and calling out to them as a friend does. "Where are you?" was his affectionate question. This question was relational and not directional (as if God didn't know where they were geographically). This personal relationship reveals a God who takes the initiative in seeking the ones he created, sustains, provides for, and loves. God is not some far-off deity who cares little for his creation, but acts as a loving parent, calling his children by name.

Throughout salvation history God continued to be with and communicate to the people he had called his own. Through signs, wonders, and the words of the prophets passed down in the written word of the Torah, God showed his love for his people. In the fullness of time, through Mary's "yes" God took on human flesh in that small town of Bethlehem. God, in the person of Jesus—fully human and fully divine—entered human history as one of us.

The Church gives us the beautiful anticipatory season of Advent to take in this divine mystery of the incarnation of God's love. During Advent, when the Church reflects what this means to our lives, we can discern that the incarnation is the inevitable expression of evangelization because love needs to be expressed, it's compelled to reveal itself to the other.

The message of evangelization is none other than God himself, God's self-disclosure in the person of Jesus Christ. A theological proposition of evangelization is that God desires to be known and can be known. "The desire for God is written in the human heart, because man is created by God and for God; and God never ceases to draw man to himself. Only in God will he find the truth and happiness he never stops searching for" (CCC, 27).

Modern man stifles God's voice with unnecessary noise so that little attention is given to the interior life. The message that we were created to live for ourselves or that joy is attained through acquiring the latest gadgets is a lie. For Christians, we don't live just once; we are created for eternal life. God's word remains and continues to speak to the human heart when we place our whole being, interior life and all, at God's disposal. Then we can begin to live.

Responding to the word of God opens us up to dialogue with others who are seeking God. This mutual experience of God provides fertile ground for us to connect with people from all walks of life. The *Catechism of the Catholic Church* tells us that, "The Church is expressing her confidence in the possibility of speaking about him to all men and with all men, and therefore of dialogue with other religions, with philosophy and science, as well as with unbelievers and atheists" (*CCC*, 39). Yes, even atheists are included in this dialogue, for the New Evangelization seeks to engage those who seek truth and the meaning in life. Thus, the New Evangelization wants to reach those who are seeking God, but have not yet come to the point of belief.

This search for truth, however, is not merely an intellectual pursuit or a spiritual path on which we hit different marks or levels of training before reaching enlightenment. Some may claim that they have spiritual practices that ensure belief in God, as if we can possess God by our own intellectual ability and cunning.

No, faith is a supernatural gift; it's a virtue that allows us to enter communion with the Holy Trinity: Father, Son, and Holy Spirit. This gift is bestowed on us by God who takes the initiative in calling us to himself. Faith is not an object to be possessed but a gift to be shared. It opens our eyes to God and allows us to see all things anew. In John's Gospel, no one comes to an understanding of Jesus on their own: the truth must be revealed to them.

The Second Vatican Council made clear that, "In His goodness and wisdom God chose to reveal Himself and to make known to us the hidden purpose of His will by which through Christ, the Word made flesh, man might in the Holy Spirit have access to the Father and come to share in the divine nature."[10] The idea of "drawing near" is at the heart of the incarnation, God drawing near to us in a way that was humble, meek, unpretentious, and relatable.

The New Evangelization seeks to "put flesh" on the Gospel message in what Pope Benedict XVI calls venturing into the "Courtyard of the Gentiles."[11] The Courtyard of the Gentiles amounts to a way for Catholicism to present the best of itself to the world. When entering into the courtyard, what we find is not always atheists and agnostics, but baptized Catholics who no longer believe. The New Evangelization is not retreating in fear from those who don't believe, but actively entering into the arenas of public discourse, social gatherings, and places of work in order to engage, discuss, and proclaim Christ with zeal.

"And the Word Became Flesh and Made His Dwelling Among Us…"

How do we "dwell among" others? We may succeed at dwelling with other Catholics and people who believe as we do, although I know in my own life there is room for improvement. Do we identify ourselves as Catholic when we are out and about? Do we mention, at appropriate times, our beliefs on current topics, our attendance at Mass, our practice of prayer or Catholic-related activities that define who we are? While it is becoming increasingly difficult to even profess a belief in God, it seems to be even more ostracizing to proclaim fidelity to the Catholic Church. Many people are afraid how others, who may be hostile to Jesus or the Church, may react. Some may feel ill-equipped to speak about and defend their faith. But as Jesus said, be not afraid!

Jesus, too, was born into a hostile environment. Recall the events surrounding his birth. Born in the shadow of King Herod's reign in Bethlehem, under Roman occupation, Jesus's life and the lives of all boys under two years of age were threatened with murder by the king. After Jesus's birth, Mary and Joseph escaped to Egypt, and we can only imagine the slaughter that took place behind them.

Throughout his short life on earth, Jesus was surrounded by enmity, even from his own people. Those in his hometown wanted to throw him out of the synagogue and off a cliff. He confronted his disciples who argued among themselves, religious leaders who tried to trap him and plot his death, and one of the twelve who would betray him. Jesus truly was a "sheep among the wolves;" unfortunately, that is still a reality today.

Nevertheless, love compels us. The truth compels us. Our encounter with the living God who loves us and gave himself for us compels us. No other reason will do. It's this love which has turned sinners and cowards into martyrs and saints. A wonderful opportunity lies before us to imitate the life of Jesus in the midst of a culture that is becoming increasingly hostile to Christ. We must be the light in a culture where there are no absolutes and no objective right or wrong. We must demand that moral rules and absolutes are not merely left to personal preference. We must bring Christ to this world.

As the Word of God became flesh and dwelt among us, we, too, are called to live out and share our faith in our daily lives. However, we do not have to face this challenge alone. We have the promise that Jesus goes with us, we have a Church that encourages us, we have the Blessed Mother in heaven praying for us, and we have the Holy Spirit with us, offering the right words at the right time.

Quote

> By the way we have lived our lives, we have represented or misrepresented God to people. What an unspeakable grave duty we have—never to give a distorted impression of God by what we do or what we say.
>
> —Msgr. James Truro

New Evangelization Connection

1. Who has "incarnated" or reflected Christ to you in your life? What qualities do they have that you would like to imitate?
2. Where is your Courtyard of the Gentiles? Think about one small step that you can take by yourself or through your parish which may open a door to speak about Christ, especially to someone who no longer believes.

Prayer

Living God, enfleshed in Jesus, may the mystery of the incarnation comfort us and encourage us as we too, enter into a world that can be hostile to God and the Church. Send your Holy Spirit to remind us that you are in charge of all evangelization and that no word spoken of your love and forgiveness is ever wasted. Nourish us with the Eucharist, the living bread from heaven, that we may become united with the one we proclaim. Amen.

CHAPTER THREE

JOHN 3

Nicodemus: Evangelization and Confrontation

. . .

Now there was a Pharisee named Nicodemus, a ruler of the Jews.

. . .

Confrontation is something that most people like to avoid. It is much easier to smile and nod at someone with whom you disagree than to speak up and enter into a conversation which will likely lead to conflict. Confronting others about their conduct or beliefs may presuppose that we have our act together, so we better be quiet and move along.

Not so if we want to make an impact for Christ. In evangelization we hear so often that we need to build a relationship with a person in order to win the right to be heard. This is a prudent way of evangelizing and it speaks to the fact that we sincerely care about the person and are not just trying to win them over to our belief. Discipleship is a lifelong process. As is evident in the story of Nicodemus, however, there is a time to confront others. In following the example of Jesus, we can do this in a way that is scriptural and loving, and allows the other to make his or her own choice.

In chapter three of John's Gospel, Jesus is confronted at night by a man named Nicodemus. Nicodemus is a Pharisee and a leader of the Jews. Many speculate that Nicodemus came to Jesus at night for fear of what the other Pharisees may have thought about his visiting this controversial rabbi from the hill country of Galilee. Should a Jerusalem-trained Pharisee be asking questions and seeking theological clarification from a rabbi who is not part of the established religious community?

There is a rabbinic tradition that may soften the view that Nicodemus acted out of fear or in secrecy. The tradition tells us that the astute Jewish student studied the Torah both day and night. Here we find Nicodemus asking questions of the living Torah, the Word of God—Jesus—at night. Thus, this was an honorable endeavor for a scholar seeking to know God. In examining Nicodemus's words we find that he is familiar with the Hebrew Scriptures, which we would expect from a Pharisee. He has a healthy respect for Jesus and he acknowledges that Jesus is from God. He was a teacher of the word of God, yet lacked understanding of God's plan and salvation.

In response to Nicodemus's praise, Jesus confronts him with a statement which hastens the direction he desires the conversation to go, "Very truly, I tell you, no one can see the kingdom of God without being born from above" (John 3:3). This leads Nicodemus to ask a question about what it means to be born again. Jesus uses this as an opportunity to explain the difference between physical and spiritual life, and the role of the Holy Spirit in God's plan for salvation. Jesus's use of the word *pneuma,* which is translated as "spirit" or "wind," has a double meaning that Nicodemus would have appreciated as it related to the natural reality of a cool breeze and the movement of God's Spirit.

Nicodemus asks another question and Jesus responds with two questions of his own. It is here that Jesus confronts Nicodemus and says bluntly, "Are you a teacher of Israel, and yet you do not understand these things?" (John 3:10). At this point in the dialogue we might shrink back and question why Jesus would say such a thing. Didn't he just shut Nicodemus down? Perhaps this says something about Jesus's view of teachers and the knowledge they should have if they are to be esteemed as such.

Jesus doesn't end on that note, however. In fact, the master teacher and evangelist then brings the conversation into a realm that Nicodemus will understand: Scripture. Jesus uses an Old Testament illustration for clarification when referencing Moses and the serpent being lifted up in the desert. He speaks for the first time the phrase, "eternal life" and emphatically professes God's love for humanity and of his own sacrificial love for the whole world. The choice is clear: salvation and eternal life in Jesus's name or eternal judgment for sin.

Jesus's confrontation with Nicodemus did have positive effects. Afterward, when the Pharisees ordered the temple officers to arrest Jesus, Nicodemus was the sole member of that group who offered a word in defense of Jesus. "Nicodemus, who had gone to Jesus before, and who was one of them, asked, 'Our law does not judge people without first giving them a hearing to find out what they are doing, does it?'" (John 7:50–51) In Nicodemus's final biblical appearance he asks for permission to take Jesus's body down from the cross and bury him (John 19:39–40) . Only love for Jesus could have moved this "secret" disciple into the public light of being known as one of his disciples.

In the process of evangelization, are we comfortable in confronting others with the same straightforwardness and love that Jesus displays? Can we point to the Scriptures with ease and familiarity, and to Jesus's effect on our own life as a way sharing with others the love we have experienced? Pope Benedict XVI reminds us, "We cannot keep to ourselves the words of eternal life given to us in our encounter with Jesus Christ: they are meant for everyone, for every man and woman.... It is our responsibility to pass on what, by God's grace, we ourselves have received." [12]

The transmission of the Christian faith begins with a transmission of a person. Seeking ways to announce and convey the person and message of Jesus is the challenge that the New Evangelization itself confronts. The presentation of the Gospel will undoubtedly lead to conflict and hostilities. This should not deter us because the Gospel of Jesus Christ reconciles us with God, liberates humanity from sin, and raises us up so we, too, can be "born from above."

The Catholic Church continues to bring people to the living waters of baptism where the baptized offer themselves to God, and have Christ formed in them (see *CCC*, 526, 537). Like Jesus, we believe in the dignity and freedom of every person and allow each to come to his or her own conclusion. The truth can't be forced but must be received by an open heart.

To confront or not confront? This question involves discernment on the seriousness of the matter at hand. In general, we need to assess the nature of our relationship with the person, the seriousness of the issue, and the desire of the other person to change. If one is generally hostile to the person doing the confronting then it is likely that nothing will change. It doesn't mean that we should not confront, but we should be aware that change is unlikely. In the Gospel accounts, only once is Jesus called honest and forthright—and this is by his enemies.

When we know confrontation is called for we should begin with an interior prayer. It is the Holy Spirit who ultimately changes hearts, our own included. It is important not to "hit and run" when confronting others. We should allow sufficient time to speak and find a place conducive to conversation. Our dialogue should be focused on the issue or theological point, and not on the other person's personality or character. Remember that disagreements will occur, but in the midst of these disagreements, we continue to love the person; that's what will separate authentic love from just trying to win the person over.

As Christ spoke with Nicodemus he didn't demand change, but he offered Nicodemus a choice and allowed him to choose. In confronting with love, we assist the other person in examining the consequences of their beliefs and behavior. Without love, we unconsciously force the other person into a defensive mode where they are closed off to the Gospel.

I think St. Paul would add that we must always confront others in truth and in joy. St. Paul wrote most of his letters in response to conflict within the Church and to protect the Church from attacks coming from outside the community. He would confront in such a way that the truth was presented with the assurance of his love and continued prayers.

Confrontation can lead to conflict in our relationships, but, as in this case of Nicodemus, it can also lead to eternal life. In our everyday lives we should pray for courage to speak of God's love.

Parishes can greatly assist by providing training in apologetics, and in helping Catholics to articulate the faith in ways that are loving, non-threatening, and life-giving. I find that when I take this challenge seriously my prayer life increases dramatically because I'm quick to realize that I am inadequate for the task. Nevertheless, Christ calls us to the challenge and will provide the words and peace that come from God alone.

Quote

Being the Catholic chaplain at a secular, state university, there doesn't seem to be a day that goes by where the Church, her teachings, values, leaders are mocked, derided or dismissed from all quarters. Initially I was wildly uncomfortable at having to interact with professors or administrators challenging or confronting them on what they've said. Yet, Jesus Christ has emboldened me to do just that. To share the truth, which he embodies and commands me to do so in love, Jesus has used me to disarm many a critic while at the same time humbling me in ways I could never imagine. Part of the joy of ministry is realizing I receive much more than I give in service.

—Fr. Jim Chern, Chaplain Montclair State University,
Director of Catholic Campus Ministry for the Archdiocese
of Newark

New Evangelization Connection

1. Think of times when you were confronted about your beliefs or actions. Was the confrontation helpful or hurtful? What could have made the confrontation more constructive?
2. Who are some people in your life you need to confront? In confronting those who have left the Church, what approach might work best?

Prayer

Lord God, it's easy to believe that we are always right and have all the answers. In our desire to lead others to your son, help us to be holy so that the confrontations we have will always reflect love for the other. Allow us to be open to being confronted by others as well, seeing all contact with people as a gift from you, leading us to be conformed in your son's image. Let us confront as Jesus did, desiring always that the truth be spoken in love. Amen.

CHAPTER FOUR

JOHN 4:7
Evangelizing the Marginalized and Outcast

. . .

A Samaritan woman came to draw water, and Jesus said to her, "Give me a drink."

. . .

One of the foundational phrases for Catholic social teaching over the past several decades is the "preferential option for the poor." However, this is not a new concept for Christians who have their spiritual roots in Judaism which also speaks of concrete actions and service towards the poor.[13] Concern for the poor was a priority for Jesus in his preaching and in his actions.

In an encyclical entitled *Deus Caritas Est,* Pope Benedict XVI writes, "Love for widows and orphans, prisoners, and the sick and needy of every kind, is as essential…as the ministry of the sacraments and preaching of the Gospel."[14] Often when I think of the needy in the synoptic Gospels, it is the materially poor who come to mind.

New Testament Greek provides a few different words which we translate as "poor," and each has a slightly different emphasis. *Ani* is the most common word, used seventy-seven times, and refers to a person who is bowed down and is dependent upon others to whom they must look for help. *Anaw* is used to describe people who feel they have little value or worth before God. *Ebyon* is used close to sixty times throughout the Bible and refers to those who are beggars. The last significant word is *ptochos,* which denotes a person who must hide away in fear. When we examine the nuances of each word, it should help expand the biblical definition of poor, which, in my opinion, was too narrowly defined for many years.

If we were to have access only to the Gospel of John, without ever reading Matthew, Mark, or Luke, I wonder if my thoughts would be the same regarding the poor? Throughout John's Gospel the poor are better characterized as those on the margins of society. While John rarely uses the word *poor* in his Gospel he does reveal Jesus's concern for the poor by focusing on those who were separated from society. He continually shows us how Jesus engages in dialogue and reaches out to those who are alienated from others. This group includes women, people who were ignorant of the law or the crowd, the physically sick, public sinners, and those who lived outside of Jerusalem. John devotes most of chapter four—forty-two verses in all—to one such marginalized person who falls into four of those five categories.

In the fourth chapter of John we read about a woman from Samaria who comes to a well to draw water. It is about the sixth hour, or noon, when she arrives. This is a particularly odd time for a woman to draw water since that task was normally completed in the early morning hours. Perhaps because of her public, sinful life, she was an object of scorn, and so decided to fetch water at a time when she would be alone. Perhaps she was not welcomed by her community.

How many people outside the Church feel welcomed and valued by our communities and at our Sunday Masses? How many baptized members of our Church feel like this woman surely did—no longer a part of the Body of Christ because of their sinful behavior, present or past? It may be easy for us to say that this woman is an obvious sinner, so she has placed herself outside the community. There may be feelings of self-righteousness in that we are the *faithful* and she is a *sinner*.

Are our judgments justified? I dare say that if we didn't allow sinners to attend Mass, there would be no one in attendance! Let's look at the situation and see how our Lord handled this public sinner. Jesus, of all people, understood the situation. What would he do as this woman came into view? If Jesus speaks at all, one might expect condemnation for this woman's lifestyle and public sins. After all, he is God. He has all the answers, and this should inform our response to others in light of the New Evangelization.

Remarkably, Jesus initiates the conversation with this Samaritan woman in a public space, from the position of *weakness*. He recognizes that she has something that he needs, and he uses that as an entrance into dialogue. Jesus plainly states, "Give me a drink." From the woman's vantage point, Jesus has two strikes against him. He is a man and a Jew. Strict Jews were not allowed to greet women, even their own spouses, in public, and Jesus was certainly prohibited from using the same vessel this woman touched. Historically, the animosity between the Jews and Samaritans only adds to the drama of this meeting. There appears to be no common ground, no reason to talk, and nothing to agree upon.

Yet Jesus teaches us an important lesson in evangelization. In spite of all the reasons why he should not have contact with her, he gets her attention not by telling her something she needs to know, but by asking her for something *he needs*. He asks for a drink of water. The dialogue that ensues begins with a question and continues as Jesus listens thoughtfully to her response. He is not quick to interrupt;

he sits and listens. How many others had listened to this woman? How many had ever asked her for anything? How many had even acknowledged her presence? Yet here she is respected and useful, maybe for the first time in her life. Jesus did not judge her—he loved her.

Jesus was not afraid to have social contact with this woman who was marginalized by society and by the religious leadership. In asking her for a drink of water, he catches her off guard. How many other religious people in her life saw her only as a sinful woman? Jesus sees her for who she really is: a daughter of God the Father. Viewing her this way, leads to acting in a way that is familial and welcoming. Jesus's willingness to cast aside cultural prejudices and labels grabs her attention, as it should our own. Jesus did not judge by outward appearance, rather, he exhibited humility in her presence.

This common interest, a drink, was a bridge that Jesus could use to break down barriers. By taking the initiative and asking a question, the dialogue could begin and then move to the heart of the matter. It began in the physical realm, water, and then Jesus moved it to the spiritual realm—living water and eternal life.

Jesus came to seek and save the lost. He did not condemn unnecessarily, but loved unconditionally. In the spirit of the New Evangelization, how difficult is it for many to begin a conversation with those who appear vastly different? How easy the temptation to lecture others on the truth of our faith and how angry we become when our efforts are mocked or dismissed. Jesus shows us by his example how to reach those across the table.

As the conversation continues, we see the woman turning the topic away from her and to the question of where one should worship. Jesus answers effectively, and subtly turns the conversation back to the original question: that of Jesus's identity and what he has to offer.

In John 4:26 Jesus confronts her with his identity, "I am he, the one who is speaking to you." Jesus reveals his identity as the Messiah only after he has laid the groundwork. The result of Jesus's conversation with this woman was the conversion of many people in the city of Sychar. She becomes an evangelist, telling others of the good news of Jesus. She invites others to "come and see."

In the work of the New Evangelization, we may experience those who are ready to hear the message, while at other times we may have to wait for the right words at the right time. Sometimes, it may take many months or even years for the groundwork of trust to be established. We don't need to be perfect before we begin the conversation, but we do need to be credible. Credibility is an invaluable tool in evangelization. As Pope Paul VI wrote in 1975, people today "are more impressed by witnesses than by teachers, and if they listen to these it is because they also bear witness."[15]

When examining how Jesus evangelized, we see that he is not afraid to engage one who is outside the community of believers. He meets the woman at the well in the everyday events of her life. Jesus sees an opportunity and seizes it. He is in a constant state of preparedness to do so. Evangelization is often a spontaneous encounter through human eyes, yet we know that God ordains every meeting. The decision to evangelize lies within our reach. As we read in 1 Peter 3:15, "Always be ready to make your defense to anyone who demands from you an accounting for the hope that is in you."

Pope John Paul II noted that the methodology of an evangelist never "imposes" but only "proposes" the truth, always respecting the freedom of the recipient to accept or reject it. When the truth of Christ and the Church is presented, it doesn't need to be imposed;

men and women are naturally attracted to it.

Finally, prayer must precede and permeate our efforts and our way of being Church in the New Evangelization. Reaching out to those beyond our personal comfort zone, to those who have left the Church, to those who no longer believe in God, may be frightening, but it is exciting. We quickly come to realize that it is not about us, but about the Holy Spirit who is moving through us to bring about conversion, hope, and joy in the lives of others. In this account recorded by John we see that the woman who is loved by Jesus becomes an evangelist, and she quickly goes to her own people and speaks about Christ. Her personal testimony is the impetus that brings the townspeople to come out to see and hear for themselves.

Let us never be afraid to reach out to those whom we might think of as far away from God. In truth, no one is ever far from the heart of the Father no matter how hard they may try to distance themselves from him. Pope Benedict XVI says: "We seek only to place ourselves at the service of all humanity, especially the suffering and the excluded, because we believe that 'the effort to proclaim the Gospel to the people of today…is a service rendered to the Christian community and also to the whole of humanity.'"[16]

Who are the people that you see on the margins and have never considered trying to reach with Christ's message? Those who are not Catholic? The divorced and separated? Those with a criminal record? College students? Homosexuals? Those who have been away from Mass for years? Whoever they may be, by examining and modeling how Jesus reached out in humility and truth, we may be able to share the love of Christ, which has so transformed us.

Quote

The occasion and the preparation of the woman was the request of Christ; thus he says, "Give me a drink." He asks for a drink both because he was thirsty for water on account of the heat of the day, and because he thirsted for the salvation of man on account of his love. Accordingly, while hanging on the cross he cried out: "I Thirst."[17]

—St. Thomas Aquinas, Commentary on the Gospel of John

New Evangelization Connection

1. Have you ever been marginalized by others? How did it feel? Did it make you angry or more empathetic towards those who have experienced the same?
2. What are some ways you can intentionally reach out to others who may be on the margins of family life, society, Church? What are some strategies that your parish can adapt to be more intentional in evangelizing those outside of the Church?

Prayer

Jesus, help us to recognize and reach out to those who are marginalized. May you open our eyes to those closest to us who are pressed down by life's burdens and give us the wisdom to recognize our own prejudices and to eliminate them. Come Holy Spirit, instill within us a courageous zeal and fortitude to challenge those who oppress others. May our dialogue in friendship instill in the marginalized a sense of God's love, presence, and purpose in their lives and may we be humble enough to learn from them. We pray this through Christ, our Lord. Amen.

CHAPTER FIVE

JOHN 5:1–9

Evangelization One Person at a Time

. . .

When Jesus saw him lying there and knew that he had been
there a long time, he said to him, "Do you want to be made
well?" The sick man answered him, "Sir, I have no one to put
me into the pool when the water is stirred up; and while I
am making my way, someone else steps down ahead of me."

. . .

It always bothered me that Jesus healed just one person that day
around the pool of Bethesda when so many were in need. My initial
reaction was to question Jesus and the use of his power to heal.
Why didn't he heal everyone that day? As time goes, by I think I'm
beginning to understand why Jesus stopped for just one person. His
decision to reach out to this one, solitary man lies at the heart of
evangelization.

We are informed that Jesus goes up to Jerusalem to attend a feast.
On his way he passes the pool—Bethesda—a word which in Hebrew
means, "house of mercy" or "house of grace." The archeological
remains of this pool were discovered in the nineteenth century and
can be seen today by those who visit Jerusalem. In antiquity, this pool
was known to be a place of healing. As we read in the story, many
ill, blind, and lame people came to the pool or were placed there by
others.

The reason this pool was thought to contain healing power lay in the fact that the water would stir and the people thought that it was the very finger of God moving the water. As we see in the story, this particular man complained about having no one to place him in the pool first. It's difficult to ascertain the exact reason why the water stirred. Some suggest that there was an intermittent spring below that would agitate the water with a surge in the flow. The pool at Siloam had a similar underground spring.

It must have been quite a scene. Perhaps ten blind people, twenty lame people, and dozens more who were sick from various diseases known and unknown in the ancient world gathered at the pool. All were there with the hope of making it into the water first, as it began to stir. I can imagine the scene when someone called out, "The water is moving, the water is moving!" The mad dash to be the first one in must have created chaos.

It is here that we are introduced to a man who had been ill for thirty-eight years. Thirty-eight years of hoping for a cure, thirty-eight years of seeking relief, thirty-eight years of agony. Whether or not he spent all that time huddled around this pool is unknown, but perhaps as a last-ditch effort the community placed him there and let him be. The pool became his only hope.

Jesus interrupts his journey to the temple because he notices this man and knows that he had been ill for a long time. Jesus stops and asks an intriguing question, "Do you want to be well?" On one hand we have to admit that this is an odd question—of course he wants to be well! Thirty years of illness and now here he is at this pool, a place where healing is sought. Still Jesus asks the question as if he knows that the answer may result in a new way of life for the sick man. The sick man does not give the traditional "yes" or "no" response, but rather says that he has no one to get him to this magical pool. Jesus commands him to "Rise, pick up your mat and walk." The man walks and a miracle has been witnessed.

I wasn't present, yet I believe this miracle took place. The Church, too, proclaims that it happened. If we can agree that it happened then we might be satisfied to say we are happy the man was healed. Yet how does this story relate to my own life, especially in light of the New Evangelization?

Here are a few points to consider. First, the only thing that has changed for most people in our culture is the pool. The question we now need to ask is, "What's *your* pool?" Like the sick man who sought healing in Bethesda, most people have a "pool" in which they say, "If I only can have X, then I will be happy!" More money, a new car, making the varsity team, meeting the man or woman of our dreams…These are all the "pools" where we seek to find fulfillment. The message is beautifully packaged, yet the promise is often far above what can ever be delivered.

There are many people today, just like the sick man from the Gospel, who long to be well, to be complete, to be loved. For those of us who know Christ, we have the assurance that nothing and no one else can satisfy the deep longing of our hearts. For those without Christ, we can see the pattern emerge in the life of someone who goes from experience to experience in search of wholeness. St. Augustine's words ring true, "You have made us for yourself, O Lord, and our heart is restless until it rests in you."[18]

Do we who know Christ desire for others to know him? This is the heart of an evangelist. Christ stops and shares himself with this man, demonstrating in power that wholeness and new life come in a relationship with the living God.

Those around the pool were ill, blind, and lame. Has much changed in the world? There are still multitudes of people who are blind: blind to the fact that they are created in the image and likeness of God; blind to their own beauty, worth, and dignity; blind to God's presence in his creation; blind to his presence in our brothers and sisters. Can we stop to share Christ and pray that their eyes may be opened? That's the heart of an evangelist.

The lame were present at Bethesda and are still present today. How many people have been crippled by the cruel words of others? How many have had their self-worth crippled and destroyed by unjust comparisons, bullying, and neglect? How many people long to reveal who they really are, but are crippled by the fear of humiliation or rejection? The truth is that the ill, blind, and crippled are all around us. We recognize that we, too, fall into that category and need the healing power of Christ.

If we are convinced that Jesus is the way, the truth, and the life, then those without Christ are missing out in our joy. Connecting them with Christ and revealing Jesus to them in a way that is unexpected is what the New Evangelization calls for. Asking a question like, "Do you want to be well?" or asking the first question that Jesus poses in John 1:38, "What are you looking for?" is a way to engage others and introduce Christ.

The story of the man at the pool in Bethesda contains perhaps the saddest words found in Scripture. They're on the lips of the sick man who says, "Sir, I have no one...." How truly alone this man was. Here he was in the holy land of Israel, in the holy city of Jerusalem, in the shadow of the temple where God's "Shekinah" or "glory" illuminates all creation here on earth. Here is a man who can utter the words, "I have no one." Tragic!

The New Evangelization calls us to open our eyes to those who might say they have no one. Most likely they won't cry out for help, yet can we befriend those we see each day? Can we stop and notice them as Jesus did? Can we share the good things God has done for us after we have accepted his love and committed ourselves to him? It's not easy. It's easier to get on a plane, fly to Israel, and walk where Jesus walked than it is to stay at home and live as Jesus lived.

As Jesus stopped for those whom he noticed in his daily life, we can be challenged to look anew at those we see each day. The care we give them in the name of Jesus puts flesh on the New Evangelization. I mentioned at the beginning that at first, I was disappointed that Jesus only healed one person that day. In retrospect, I'm glad that Jesus healed just one. It provides for me a realistic goal in evangelizing others. I certainly don't have to heal the world, but I can make the effort to reach out to one person. As Mother Teresa said, "If you can't feed one thousand people, just feed one."[19]

Jesus noticed a person in need, he stopped, talked with him, and did what he could. The New Evangelization needs us to see like Jesus, to shift our perspective, and to see people and circumstances through the lens of faith. With the Holy Spirit at your side, imagine how exciting tomorrow will be as you approach the day and the people you meet with the eyes of Christ.

Quote

But let us not put our sights too high. We do not have to be saviours of the world! We are simply human beings, enfolded in weakness and in hope, called together to change our world one heart at a time.[20]

—Jean Vanier

New Evangelization Connection

1. The New Evangelization calls for a mind-set that seeks out those who are lost. How does your parish intentionally reach out to those who are blind to the presence of Jesus?

2. Jesus reached out to one person among the many. How can we reflect the truth that the Gospel is spread one person at a time?

Prayer

Lord Jesus, slow us down each day and allow us to see life through your eyes. May we never bypass the individual in need, whether they cry out or sit in silence. Give us the grace at the beginning of each day to reflect on what is really important, and the knowledge that all of our encounters are ordained by your providence. Open our eyes to one person on the margins today, the one too proud or weak to ask for help. Holy Spirit, come to our aid and make us more like Jesus. Amen.

CHAPTER SIX

JOHN 7:53—8:11
In Mercy and Truth

. . .

Jesus straightened up and said to her, "Woman, where are
they? Has no one condemned you?" She said, "No one, sir."
And Jesus said, "Neither do I condemn you. Go your way,
and from now on do not sin again."

. . .

There is power in walking around with a weapon. These weapons
can take the form of guns or knives, but more often than not they
consist of our words. These "stones" can give us a level of comfort
in case someone should threaten us. In this story of Jesus and the
woman caught in adultery, we gain beautiful insight into the mercy
of God. We learn an invaluable lesson in how Jesus extends his love
to a woman who is caught in sin without using any stones of violence,
but words of mercy and truth.

Not all who were present that day were adulterers, and not all those
present wanted this woman killed. Jesus had come to the temple to
teach. However, he was soon caught up in a plan of entrapment by
the scribes and Pharisees. They used this sinful woman as their ploy
to accuse Jesus. Their motives were anything but pure.

This story reads beautifully as a three-act play, in which a human
life hangs in the balance. The scribes and Pharisees enter the stage as

Jesus is teaching and try to trap him with a question. Jesus responds with an unprecedented action and a bold proclamation. The scribes and Pharisees exit stage left leaving Jesus alone with the woman, who awaits his closing remarks.

As we examine the behavior of the religious leaders, we read that their intention is to discredit Jesus, putting him at odds with either the Romans or the Torah. The religious leaders see only two answers to their questions. If Jesus sanctions the stoning, the Romans will arrest him, for only the Romans were authorized to administer and conduct capital punishment. On the other hand, if Jesus prohibits the stoning of the woman, the Pharisees will accuse him of contradicting the Torah, the Law of Moses. Thus, the trap is set. While we read this passage we are challenged to see whom we align ourselves with: Jesus, the woman, the religious leaders, or the crowd.

The woman, known only by her sin, was humiliated by the scribes and Pharisees. She was publicly accused of a serious sin and was condemned by the religious leaders who were eagerly waiting with stones in hand. This is in stark contrast to Jesus who appears calm. He did not act frantic, nor was he panicked. He was not moved by the self-righteous religious leaders.

Rather than examine the woman, Jesus bends down and writes in the sand. He takes the attention away from this woman, at least momentarily. In proposing the statement, "Let anyone among you who is without sin be the first to throw a stone at her," Jesus asks the religious leaders to examine themselves. In bending down to write again he gave them time to think, time to examine their consciences. Jesus then casts his gaze upward at the woman and asks, "Woman, where are they? Has no one condemned you?" She responds by saying, "No one."

Jesus was patient with this woman. He questioned her not about her sin, but about the change of heart of the crowd. He looked up at her, recognizing that she too is created in the image and likeness of God. She felt acceptance by Jesus and received the forgiveness that would make her whole. Jesus had watched the treatment of this woman, he heard the charge against her, he knew the penalty recommended for her, yet he chose not to further humiliate her.

There will always be a tension and interior struggle in the Christian who seeks to share the love of God with others, yet does not want to condone sinful actions. Jesus affirms that adultery is a sin, yet he affirms the woman through his acceptance and forgiveness. He allows her to respond to his question in her own voice, a voice which the religious leaders denied. Jesus restores her dignity by allowing her to express the reality at hand.

How do we evangelize others while recognizing our own imperfections? Is it an act of charity to keep our mouths shut when we clearly see sinful behavior which, by definition, is harmful to the person? Have Christians ceased to speak out for fear that the crowd might challenge our own behavior and use Jesus's words against us? "He who is without sin…." While we're not casting stones, of course, has the argument been surrendered because of what the crowd may say? Is any behavior acceptable because "God is love," and our culture understands love as a feeling rather than a personification in the sacrificial life of Jesus? In a culture which denies the existence of sin, how do we present the Gospel which seeks to save us from sin? These are questions we must grapple with as we move forward with the New Evangelization.

Now let's examine a few observations from Jesus's interaction with the crowd. First, we must not judge others by the way people treat them or by the way people talk about them. Just because they may be someone's enemy does not mean that they are God's enemy. We must never humiliate or join in condemnation. It may make us feel good about ourselves, but it does nothing to bring the person into a relationship with Jesus.

We can offer to bring them to Christ as he is present in the sacrament of reconciliation, although this is not a likely starting point for a person who has left the Church or who no longer believes. The graces available through this sacrament and the reality that Jesus himself forgives the person continue to set people free. Jesus trusted that the Holy Spirit would convict people of their sinfulness and that their conscience would speak to their disordered actions and thoughts. In doing so we are acting like Jesus who treated this woman with acceptance and respect. When we encourage others to examine their lives, we are also examining our own lives.

The scribes and Pharisees brought this woman to the feet of Jesus for condemnation, but found him more interested in forgiveness than judgment. Evangelization allows Jesus to overwhelm sinful people with his love and forgiveness. Is this the Jesus we humbly portray? When the culture is anti-Christian, anti-Catholic, it is easy to adopt an us-against-them attitude. Jesus doesn't submit to this attitude and neither should we.

These realities provide some opportunities to introduce Jesus as he is presented in Scripture. He forgave the woman and he loved her, yet he was adamant that she go and sin no more. The task of presenting anew the person of Jesus is at the heart of the New Evangelization. Those who have left Christ or his Church and have come back rediscover the power of a personal relationship with him. When they return and discover the fullness of the faith in the Scripture and the tradition of the Catholic Church, their eyes are opened, and they long to deepen their faith.

There are enough people with stones in their hands ready to hurl away. Let us adopt the example of Jesus who, at every occasion, seeks to wrap the individual in love and calls them to a life of holiness.

Quote

We are not at peace with others because we are not at peace with ourselves, and we are not at peace with ourselves because we are not at peace with God.[21]

—Thomas Merton

New Evangelization Connection

1. Jesus was watched by the crowd to see how he would react. Are there instances in your life where you were Christ-like? Are there moments in the past where you wish you could have a do-over?
2. This woman was brought to Jesus and publicly humiliated. How can your parish actively help those whose dignity has been wounded and assist them on the road to recovery? How can you assist with those who have been wounded by the Church?

Prayer

Lord, so often we find ourselves with stones in hand ready to throw them at those who mock and reject you. Allow your way of peace and nonviolence to permeate our hearts and relax our grip so that the stones may fall by the wayside and we may embrace and lift others up. Let us creatively reach out to those who have fallen and show them the forgiveness of Christ in our actions and through the sacrament of reconciliation. We pray this in Jesus's name. Amen.

CHAPTER SEVEN

JOHN 11:38-44
Power to Bring New Life

. . .

So they took away the stone…. And Jesus raised his eyes and said, "Father, I thank you for having heard me. I know that you always hear me; but I have said this for the sake of the crowd standing here, so that they may believe that you sent me." When he had said this, he cried out in a loud voice, "Lazarus, come out!" The dead man came out, his hands and feet bound with strips of cloth, and his face wrapped in a cloth. So Jesus said to them, "Unbind him and let him go."

. . .

Jesus was not afraid to reach out to sinners: to women and men, to the sick, to the scribes and Pharisees, and in this story his reach extends beyond the grave. Jesus does not always act alone, however. In this story he is first informed of the illness by Mary and Martha, and then assisted by the unnamed stone movers who remove the stone and unwrap the bandages. For Jesus, his work is speaking his word.

The story of the raising of Lazarus is traditionally the last sign Jesus performs in John's Gospel. The first sign was turning water into wine at the wedding at Cana. There are a few connections between these two miracle stories, for the first and last signs are explicitly linked with the revelation of God's glory. All of Jesus's signs were revelations of who he is and what he offers. The final sign, the raising of Lazarus, points clearly to what has been at the heart of the revelation: Jesus is the one who gives life.

The paradox, of course, is that Jesus gives life by giving up his own life on the cross. Another irony is that by restoring life to Lazarus, Jesus sets in motion the design of his enemies which will lead to his own death. The raising of Lazarus is the final sign before the cross, which accomplishes what all the previous signs point toward: the grace of resurrected life through the death of the Son of God.

This story also continues to develop the theme of faith. Jesus's love for Lazarus and his sisters teaches that our faith in God's love, even in the midst of suffering, is well-founded. When Jesus heard the news of Lazarus's death, he said, "This illness does not lead to death; rather it is for God's glory, so that the Son of God may be glorified through it" (John 11:4). This response sets the stage and provides the approach to what will follow, similar to the stories of the blind man and the sick man at Bethesda. Both ended with God being glorified.

A Jewish text that cites an authority from the early third century AD states that the mourners should continue to come to the tomb for three days because the dead person continues to be present. They believed that the soul may hover over the body for three days and then depart.[22]

The mention of the days emphasizes that Lazarus was dead. Jesus approaches the tomb and is perturbed. His anger is not at a lack of faith, but at death and its opposition to him as life-giver. Jesus came to the tomb in this state of anger ready to exercise his power over death. This begins the process that will lead to his own death and final victory over death. Christ does not come to the tomb of Lazarus as a bystander, but as an active participant. He is like an athlete preparing for the match that lies ahead.

Jesus asks some nameless onlookers to move the stone. It is as if before the Son of God defeats man's greatest foe—death—Jesus asks for help. Before Lazarus responds to the word of Jesus and comes from death to life, Jesus asks for help to move a stone.

The labor involved in pre-evangelization is much like the labor of those stone movers. Building relationships in friendship and trust so that we may begin to address any impediments to belief can be difficult, but it is necessary. Many believe that the Church and Catholics have lost credibility. The work of teaching, and helping to move intellectual and emotional stones that can be stumbling blocks for accepting Jesus, can take time. While this may seem overwhelming, just think of the converts who needed the time and assistance of others before they came to Christ or came into communion with the Catholic Church.

In this regard I am thankful to my mother who early on moved my stones of childhood ignorance of God and opened the door for me to hear the word of God. I'm grateful for those countless religious education teachers whose names I've forgotten, who helped impart some aspect of theology and love of Jesus in my formation. We, like the stone movers, listen to Jesus and do what we can to help others be open to him. The body of Christ, working together, can be a powerful force in moving the stones that block the way to presenting the word of Christ.

The image of a dead body suits our current culture of death well—a culture that declares God dead yet yearns for life and joy that comes from God alone: a culture that idolized celebrities yet destroys the unborn child in the womb. The people we meet on a daily basis are alive physically, but more often than not, they are dead spiritually.

Jesus prays aloud a prayer of thanksgiving. He directly tells Lazarus to "Come out!" Lazarus comes out tied hand and foot with burial bands, his face wrapped with a cloth. In the story, Lazarus immediately appears at the entrance, yet anyone who has visited the tomb of Lazarus knows there are nine winding steps that must be negotiated in order climb out.

My point is that after Jesus commanded Lazarus to come out, it must have taken sixty to ninety seconds for Lazarus, bound hand and foot, to climb out. What was the crowd thinking during that minute and a half? The crowd was astonished that Jesus talked this way, but that was Jesus proclaiming his word. It is a word that brought life two thousand years ago to a man named Lazarus in the village of Bethany, and it continues to have the power to bring life to those who respond in faith today.

After Lazarus comes out, the work is not done, for we are told that Jesus commands them to untie him and let him go. The New Evangelization is not just getting people to say "yes" to Jesus, as if that is the goal in our evangelizing efforts. We do not believe in a once-saved-always-saved mentality. The Church calls us to lifelong discipleship. This is exemplified in the actions of the nameless servants who help untie Lazarus. Even though Lazarus is alive, there are bands that bind him and a cloth that covers his face, rendering him blind.

In a similar way, what binds us? Unrepented sin? An unhealthy self-esteem? A distorted image of God? A prejudiced attitude? All of these "bonds" can keep us from being authentic evangelists. We need the humility to ask others, such as spiritual directors, what we need to let go of in order to be free. Just like the sinful woman in Luke 7:35–50, we need to pour out our former way of life at Jesus's feet so we can be filled with him.

Only when we have placed ourselves before Jesus and are in a state of grace can we gently assist others in the task of unbinding. Spiritual direction, Scripture study, service to others, the sacrament of reconciliation, and prayer are a few of the tools that can assist us in helping others begin and sustain lifelong discipleship. The ways and means that we use to assist people must be carefully and prayerfully administered. In this spirit, we may assist Jesus in his work of calling others out of darkness and death into the light of Jesus.

Quote

When I tell Christians that I'm an agnostic, I get a few different responses. From some I get a series of biblical quotations and never hear from them again; others give me a look of pity, but most remain silent and no longer talk to me. There are one or two, however, who continue to be my friend despite my questioning nature. In the course of time they have asked me questions about my beliefs and provided some reasons why they believe. Whether I come to believe in God or Jesus or not, I know that through their friendship I can at least feel comfortable to ask the big questions.

—James R. Rufus, agnostic and friend

New Evangelization Connection

1. Reflect on those people who have assisted you in your conversion and ongoing formation. Let them know how thankful you are and that you're praying for them.
2. The stone movers and bandage removers did their work silently, without a word. Where can you assist in evangelization behind the scenes at your parish? In what situations can you bring the word of God to others?

Prayer

Jesus, Word of God, Author of Life, draw us to meditate on your tomb to experience the power of your resurrection. Let us never be afraid to reach out with your Word to those who are far away from you and spiritually dead. Renew our confidence that your word brings life, hope, and love to a fallen world that so desperately needs your presence. Inspire us to humbly move stones and remove bandages so that the power of our witness may open doors to proclaim your love that breathes life into every soul. Mary, be our guide. Amen.

CHAPTER EIGHT

LUKE 5:27–32

Calling Others to Discipleship

. . .

After this he went out and saw a tax collector named Levi, sitting at the tax booth; and he said to him, "Follow me." And he got up, left everything, and followed him.

Then Levi gave a great banquet for him in his house; and there was a large crowd of tax collectors and others sitting at the table with them. The Pharisees and their scribes were complaining to his disciples, saying, "Why do you eat and drink with tax collectors and sinners?" Jesus answered, "Those who are well have no need of a physician, but those who are sick; I have come to call not the righteous but sinners to repentance."

. . .

Imagine if Jesus used a search committee and focus group and had a series of risk management assessments for every disciple he was thinking of asking to follow him. I know—it would be purgatory. OK...hell! He would still be on earth looking for the perfect disciple. Thankfully, Jesus provides an example of calling others in freedom and spontaneity.

Jesus takes the initiative in going out into the town and calling the tax collector, Levi. He must have recognized a quality about the man that was crucial to discipleship. While others were used to identifying the man with his trade, which was scandalous to his fellow Jews, Jesus saw beyond that and perhaps noticed the value of Levi not caring what others thought. That bold characteristic is needed in one who is going to follow Christ in any age. If Levi could stand the snide remarks and sarcastic comments from his own people and still show his face in the marketplace, maybe he was tough enough to be a disciple. If our self-worth only comes from what others think, then we are useless to God as evangelists.

The word used for *follow* in Greek is *akoloutheo*. It's used as a verb seventy-three times in the Gospels to refer to being a disciple of Jesus. The imperative mode used here is reflective more of a command than of an invitation. Jesus was not saying, "Would you like to follow me?" It is also used in the present tense, which indicates Jesus was not just commanding the beginning of an action, but its habitual continuation: lifelong discipleship.

Levi left everything and followed Jesus. He followed the path of Peter, James, and John who also left everything—boats, nets, fish—to follow Jesus. Levi's action was more costly than that of Peter, James, or John, however. Levi would not be able to go back to collecting taxes, while the others could have gone back to fishing. Levi's response was dramatic in that all ties were cut. In a sense, Levi figuratively smashed his boats and tore his nets. The Jews would never hire him because of his collaboration with the Romans, and the Romans would never give him a second chance after he abandoned his post. Levi staked absolutely everything on Jesus. Christ was his only option.

This command of Jesus was not just to follow, but "Follow me." The usage in Greek signifies that Levi wasn't just a follower but one who followed *with* Jesus, a coworker or "fellow laborer," as St. Paul would say. This command from Christ to walk alongside him was accepted by Levi, changing him and the shape of history forever. This story is recorded in all three synoptic Gospels. Levi is also called Matthew, the traditional author of the first Gospel in the New Testament.

The call of Levi becomes a model for the New Evangelization both in the boldness of Christ calling to discipleship someone outside the established religious community, and in the generous response of Levi, for he gave all to Jesus. This call to follow comes to individuals but also to cultures, as then-Cardinal Ratzinger wrote:

> [The Gospel] is addressed, not merely to the individuals, but to the culture itself.... Evangelization is not simply adaptation to the culture, either; nor is it dressing up the gospel with elements of the culture, along the lines of a superficial notion of inculturation that supposes that, with modified figures of speech...the job is done.
>
> Faith is acquainted with bridge-building; it accepts what is good; but it is also a sign of opposition to whatever in the culture bars the door against the gospel.... Therefore, it has always been critical of culture also, and it must continue fearlessly and steadfastly to critique culture, especially today.... Easy compromises benefit no one.[23]

"Easy compromises benefit no one." These are strong words from the Holy Father. Jesus was uncompromising in his call to Levi, and Levi was uncompromising in his response. Through this radical discipleship, one person at a time, culture can be changed.

As a Church, we already have structures and institutions that can give life to the New Evangelization. Through catechetical programs, the sacraments of initiation, the RCIA, Catholic schools, Catholic radio, television, and social media outlets, the New Evangelization can guide those who have turned to Jesus Christ, or those who have returned to the road of discipleship, educating the former and welcoming back the latter into the Christian community. Evangelization can nourish the faithful through teaching the faith, celebrating the sacraments, and performing works of charity. The challenge may be to refocus our existing institutions as a means to introduce the person of Jesus Christ and model what it means to follow Jesus.

Like Christ, can we identify people who would have within them the seeds of radical discipleship? Can we challenge people to be as committed to Christ as they are to their jobs or favorite sports teams? The New Evangelization calls us to seek and rekindle the fire of faith in those who no longer belong to a parish or who have no active relationship with Jesus, yet have been baptized and confirmed.

Now we are getting to the heart of the New Evangelization. It's difficult to put aside our feelings about those who don't care about the Church, religion, or God. It's tough not to condemn those who are Catholic yet live their lives apart from Christ with no regard for the Church. It's easier to gather with like-minded friends and praise Jesus than to seek and call those who are lapsed. Pope John Paul II spoke of this in 1983, when he first presented the idea of a New Evangelization; this is what Pope Benedict XVI is commanding us to do now, and this is who we must become as Church.

The process of the New Evangelization is a sustained incentive to mission, which sends all Christ's disciples to proclaim the Gospel in word and deed, recognizing that our own backyard is mission territory.

Through discernment, the Church needs to discover new ways to transmit the faith to a generation who has received grace through the sacraments of initiation. This grace, however, needs to be stimulated, aroused, called forth, and enkindled in many communities.

The goal of the New Evangelization is to bring people more than just knowledge, communication skills, and tools. We must bring them to the person of Jesus. Our desire must stem from a genuine love of Christ, who desires to bring all into relationship with him for eternal salvation. If we impart knowledge, communications skills, or techniques without this passion, we fall short of our goal. We must freely and enthusiastically give what we have received for free. "From the very origins of the Church the disciples of Christ strove to convert men to faith in Christ as the Lord; not, however, by the use of coercion or of devices unworthy of the Gospel, but by the power, above all, of the word of God."[24]

Levi was commanded to follow, and he did, out of his own free will. He could have said no and stayed at his post making a comfortable living. The word of Jesus struck him at his core and Jesus became his only option. Levi had no idea where he was going, but he did know who he was going with, and so do we.

The future of the Catholic Church may look depressing at times when we read that sacramental statistics are down in almost every category, or that parish and school closings are on the rise. These facts make us increasingly aware of our failures. Yet we are a people of hope and trust, and we know that the Catholic Church has gone through even greater struggles in the past and has come out stronger for it. These challenging times can yield great fruits—more saints! Holy men, women, and children are responding to Jesus's command to come and follow every day. Like Levi, let us follow the example of so many holy people and strive to walk the road to sainthood.

Quote

Jesus, the master evangelist, had a magnetism about him. Two words were enough to draw Matthew: "Follow me." Immediately, Matthew left everything behind—his taxes, his reputation, his wealthy friends. He could never go back. And in his joy, he threw a party for Jesus.

In the measure that I am filled with Jesus, the same magnetic draw will be there for others. The deeper my relationship with the Master Evangelist, the more joyful I will be, and the stronger will be the pull for others to likewise follow him. I only need to be a willing and transparent evangelist.

—Sister Mary Joseph Schultz, S.C.C.

New Evangelization Connection

1. Who has called you to a deeper relationship with Jesus and the Church?
2. Is there a St. Paul, a Dorothy Day, or an Augustine among your friends or acquaintances? Ask the Holy Spirit to bring to mind some unlikely candidates for discipleship. Step out in faith and invite them to follow Christ. Be with them as you assist them in their spiritual walk.

Prayer

Jesus, you were straightforward and direct when you called Levi to discipleship. Open our eyes to the "Levis" in our lives who you desire to call to yourself through our invitation. Let us never dismiss others because of their occupation, appearance, or past sins. May we see within each person the saint that they are called to be. Give us courage to lead them in following you. Amen.

. . .

Why do you call me "Lord, Lord," and do not do what I tell you? I will show you what someone is like who comes to me, hears my words, and acts on them. That one is like a man building a house, who dug deeply and laid the foundation on rock; when a flood arose, the river burst against that house but could not shake it, because it had been well built. But the one who hears and does not act is like a man who built a house on the ground without a foundation. When the river burst against it, immediately it fell, and great was the ruin of that house.

. . .

We can examine this parable on multiple levels. It can be read as a simple tale, accessible to children, teaching them the importance of building a strong foundation of prayer and study to grow in their faith. We can also take it to a secondary level and see the rich theological tradition that lies behind what Jesus was revealing about himself. Let's take a deeper a look at where this tradition, which dates back to the Old Testament, comes from and it how it affected the lives of the original audience of this story.

Matthew includes this parable at the conclusion of Jesus's Sermon on the Mount, while Luke includes it here at the end of Jesus's

Sermon on the Plain. Matthew emphasizes the contrast between the wise man and the foolish man, one building on rock and the other building on sand. Luke, however, makes a distinction between having a foundation versus having no foundation. To those who first heard this parable, the reference to the foundation might have made them think back to the words of the prophet Isaiah:

> Therefore hear the word of the Lord, you scoffers
>   who rule this people in Jerusalem.
> Because you have said, "We have made a covenant with
>   death,
>   and with Sheol we have an agreement;
> when the overwhelming scourge passes through
>   it will not come to us;
> for we have made lies our refuge,
>   and in falsehood we have taken shelter";
> therefore thus says the Lord GOD,
> See, I am laying in Zion a foundation stone,
>   a tested stone,
> a precious cornerstone, a sure foundation:
>   "One who trusts will not panic."
> And I will make justice the line,
>   and righteousness the plummet;
> hail will sweep away the refuge of lies,
>   and waters will overwhelm the shelter.
> Then your covenant with death will be annulled,
>   and your agreement with Sheol will not stand;
> when the overwhelming scourge passes through
>   you will be beaten down by it. (Isaiah 28:14–18)

In both the passage from Isaiah and from Luke, we can identify two houses, as well as a water or storm reference. Likewise, the foundation is a central concern in each passage, and in each we are called to "hear the word." With the verse in Isaiah in mind, Jesus subtly changes a few of the details, which challenges his listeners to make a decision.

In the passage from Isaiah, there are two structures being described. The first is a complete building that is washed away while the second is not yet realized: it's a promise for the future. While Isaiah tells us to hear the "word of the Lord," Jesus tells us to, "hear and do my words." This is a bold Christological statement by Jesus, which is not lost on those who originally heard him. He is comparing himself, making his words equal, to God. Either Jesus is God or a he is a liar.

In the passage from Isaiah, the criticism is on having faith in Egypt and Egypt's gods instead of the Lord. Jesus criticizes those who listen and do not act on his words. The cornerstone described in Isaiah is the sure foundation. The sure foundation and the rock are the person and words of Jesus. The listener must make a choice. Do I accept Jesus and his word as the new foundation of faith? Acceptance is described not as an intellectual assent to truth alone, but through action and by doing the words of Jesus.

What I once imagined was required to dig a foundation in the Middle East is far different from what I now know it to be, after three separate study experiences in Israel. Not that I thought Jesus would start up the tractor and use hydraulics to dig, but I grossly underestimated the labor, sweat, and time it takes to build a foundation on the dry, hard clay of the Middle East. It is important to mention this because Jesus compares hearing and doing, which sounds reasonably easy, to the labor involved in digging through hard clay down to bedrock to lay the foundation.

During my time in Israel I discovered that, in biblical times, foundations were built in the summer to avoid the rain and occasional snowstorms. Even so, the tools available for digging made it a difficult task at best, and with the hot sun beating down on your head, the temptation to dig down just a few feet rather than to rock was strong. And since most homes were simple one-story edifices, it was easy to take a shortcut and think that the hard clay would suffice to hold up the walls and roof.

But then, the winter rains would come, with small trickles of water quickly turning into streams of flowing mud and surging water. As the waters rose they would eat away at the clay below the house and soften it up, thus compromising the foundation. Ultimately the whole structure would come tumbling down.

Like a house in the Middle East, our own unseen foundations are at rest when life is calm, safe, and predictable. When a storm hits, however, our lives are susceptible to destruction if not built on a firm foundation.

This parable also functions as a warning to those who trust in the shallowness of their institutions, based on corruption and collaboration with Herod and Rome, and foreshadows the storm that lies ahead for the people of Jesus's day. It shows a way out of the storm, with the offer of a new foundation in the person of Jesus Christ. The word of the Lord in Isaiah mirrors the words of Jesus. Jesus is the new Temple, the new living foundation on which we are called to build our faith.

What does this parable mean for the New Evangelization? Over the past fifty years, the Church has made wonderful advancements in many areas including Scripture studies, social justice initiatives, increased opportunities for the laity, and the growth of new ecclesial communities. Each of these can help us deepen our knowledge of Jesus.

Knowledge of Jesus is the firm foundation on which we must build our lives. Without the knowledge that there is a God, without the knowledge that God loves us, without the knowledge of what true love is, without the knowledge of the sacraments Christ gave the Church, without the knowledge of Christ's true presence in the Eucharist, without knowing that God may be unpredictable but never unfaithful, we will get washed away.

This metaphor extends to our relationship with our children, as well. As the father of three young daughters I want to exert the effort to give them a firm foundation, to be present with them, to pray with and for them, and to reveal to them the greatest love ever known: the love of God as revealed through Jesus Christ. As we look at who we are as family, the domestic church, can we dig deeper? As families, do we make praying with each other a priority? Do we celebrate special feast days together and celebrate each other's gifts? Do we look for opportunities to encourage right behavior and affirm each other lovingly?

When I visit a parish for a speaking engagement or while on vacation, I like to read the bulletin to see what the parish offers. How many activities are geared toward adult faith-formation? Social activities are important but do they supersede catechesis? Do they have to be mutually exclusive? Should all gatherings in the Church have a catechetical moment? How can we reach out to others to share the faith if we aren't sure of what our faith teaches? The teachings of our faith are so powerful that they converted St. Augustine and Dorothy Day, motivated Mother Teresa of Calcutta to work among the poor and dying, and provided the rock the saints held onto as their own sure foundation.

In a recent survey of faith-sharing activities by Australian churches, the people who identified themselves as most likely to share their faith also identified themselves as the ones who were growing in their faith.[25] This survey, which cuts across all Christian denominations, speaks to the heart of what it means to walk the walk in order to talk to the talk.

There are any number of ways to grow in love and knowledge of Jesus Christ. This parable reveals that it is hard work, but it is work with an eternal payoff: salvation. In the work of the New Evangelization, let's share the richness of the faith we have received as a gift. Let's go deep with people and not shy away from the challenging teachings or the unpopular truths of our faith. For it is in going deeper with others that we give the greatest gift: the firm foundation of a life rooted in Christ.

Quote

> Much of ministry and work is about relationships rather than programs. To be effective at your work, you need to take the time to get to know people which is in itself a sign of respect and it builds a foundation of trust. As a leader in my workplace, I try to get to know someone first and work with them second. This takes more time but in the end is worth it because all great ministry uses the gifts of not just one but a number of individuals.
>
> —Michael St. Pierre, President,
> Morris Catholic High School

New Evangelization Connection

1. Examine your Catholic foundation: your prayer life, time spent reading Scripture, your sacramental life, your service to others. Are there areas where you need to "dig deeper"?

2. Jesus speaks of hearing and doing. Are there areas in your life where you can improve how you keep these commands? Find a friend who can help keep you accountable in these areas.

Prayer

Heavenly Father, it can be easy to take shortcuts and follow the path of least resistance. In our faith journey, strengthen us as we choose the more difficult path, as we dig deeper. May we never grow tired in building our foundation of faith, and when the storms of life crash around us, may we bear witness to your love and salvation to those without faith. May our strength invite others to have Jesus as their sure foundation. We ask this through Christ our Lord. Amen.

CHAPTER TEN

LUKE 8:4–8

Sowing Seeds, Preparing Soil

. . .

When a great crowd gathered and people from town after town came to him, he said in a parable:

"A sower went out to sow his seed; and as he sowed, some fell on the path and was trampled on, and the birds of the air ate it up. Some fell on the rock; and as it grew up, it withered for lack of moisture. Some fell among thorns, and the thorns grew with it and choked it. Some fell into good soil, and when it grew, it produced a hundredfold." As he said this, he called out, "Let anyone with ears to hear listen!"

. . .

In most of the English translations of the Bible, each passage has a heading. These headings make finding a particular story easy, especially for the person who is just becoming acquainted with the Bible. In Luke 15, for example, we have three parables spoken by Jesus that are called "Lost Sheep," "Lost Coin," and "Lost Son" or sometimes "Prodigal Son." Immediately upon seeing the title we begin to recall the story.

Not to be too scrupulous, but I often think that a few of these headings mistakenly emphasize the wrong aspect of the parable. In the three examples cited above from the Gospel of Luke, I think that the emphasis is not so much on the "lostness" of the sheep, coin, and Son, but rather on the seeking nature of the shepherd, woman, and father, and the costly demonstration of unexpected love.

The parable that heads this chapter is usually referred to as the Parable of the Sower or the Sower and the Seed. Putting some emphasis on the different types of soil, rather than simply on the sower and the seed, is important for a greater understanding of this story. The sower plants the seeds in places where you would expect little or no growth at all. The soil makes the difference! In fact, in three of the four places mentioned in the parable—along the path, on rocky ground, and among thorns—one would expect little or no growth, yet the sower plants the seeds there anyway.

As we hear this parable, we might envision our own backyard garden or the cornfields of Nebraska. In the Middle East during biblical times, however, farming was much different. The rolling terrain of Galilee required that the hills be fortified and braced with retaining walls, lest the rainwater wash the soil away. The distance between these walls varied, but in most cases there were between thirty and fifty yards of real estate to farm.

The sower didn't dig a hole or a row and plant the seed, as is common to our backyard gardening. Rather, he gathered up his robe to make a pouch and placed a large amount of seed in it. He would then walk down the path and broadcast the seed to the left, to the right, and in front of him in a sweeping motion. This is the image the first hearers of this parable had in their minds as they listened to Jesus speak.

We might think it profitable only to sow in the areas where we can expect growth. Why would time and seed be wasted by allowing the seed to fall along the path, on rocky ground, and among the thorns?

The soil in which it is planted is vital to a seed's success. Why would seed be spent in areas that don't seem conducive to growth?

This parable speaks beautifully to the task of the New Evangelization: proclaiming the word of God to all people, but especially to those from whom we least expect a response. We must take the good news to those we may have written off, or to those who we are sure would never be involved in the Church or anything the least bit spiritual. Christ ends the parable with the exhortation, "Whoever has ears to hear ought to hear." All deserve to hear the word of God.

Within this parable there are a few theological points that will help encourage and guide those who are actively doing the work of evangelization. Jesus chooses an image—sowing seed in anticipation of a crop—that demands patience. There is nothing instantaneous about farming: the process is slow and steady. Certain elements are necessary for growth, like water, air, light, and nutrients, but most of all, time is needed for the seed to break open and begin to flourish, rising slowly through the soil to crack the earth. The growth that is visible above the soil is a result of the growth that is invisible, below the earth.

Discipleship is the same. The process of becoming mature in Christ and bringing others to this maturity takes time, years even, and it's a process where we are always called to grow in faith.

Jesus says that the seed *fell* upon the path: It was not *forced* into the soil. The word of God must be received into an open heart, and not one that is hardened. There is nothing more frustrating than to see a person of good intention try to force God's word into someone. It never has worked that way and never will. We are responsible for sowing the word, the proclamation, and we must then allow the Holy Spirit to handle the rest. Only God can prepare a heart to accept his love.

In this parable the sower is fully aware of the impediments to growth. We, too, evangelize with our eyes open to the obstacles—the thorns and rocky ground that can consume people's lives. Recognizing these impediments does not prevent us from being evangelists, however. Others may think we're crazy, but we must continue to sow anyway. Someone may have had a bad experience with the Church: sow anyway. Someone may post anti-Christian sentiments on his or her social networking pages: sow anyway. Sow faithfully with joy, hope, and love, and pray that the Holy Spirit may soften the hearts of those to whom you minister.

This parable can greatly encourage us as evangelists, for it guarantees a harvest. It encourages the sower not to neglect those unexpected places—people—where we think growth or acceptance is not possible. There is assurance of a great harvest, a "hundredfold!" Those individuals who do respond and become disciples may then themselves begin to sow the seed of the word of God, and have an impact far beyond what we might ever imagine. One person on fire for Christ can make an enormous difference.

The image Jesus puts forth is one of a humble barley field, not a seed of a giant sequoia or magnificent cedar of Lebanon. The image of the kingdom speaks to the ordinary and not the extraordinary. The labor is not glamorous; in fact, it's laborious, dirty work. Those who may want to evangelize in order to receive recognition have the wrong motive. Our motive must be love and we must be willing to stick our necks out like the early evangelists, Priscilla and Aquila (see Romans 16:3–4). Archbishop Fisichella, president of the Pontifical Council for the New Evangelization, spoke about the cost of evangelizing: "For Christ, to evangelize was a compulsion to which he gladly succumbed, even to the point of accepting the final result of his preaching: suffering and death. Such is the consistency of the true evangelizer: to prove that the truth of his message is worth dying for, since it is the fruit of a mission given by God."[26]

Finally, this parable illustrates that grace is operative through the actions of the sower. The soil does not work for the seed but receives it as a gift. This is grace. The sower's actions are the means by which grace is conferred, and it awaits a response. As with plants, people operate on different timetables. Some seeds remain buried deep within the soil for years before they take root. Other seeds lie dormant until conditions are right to break through the ground. The responsibility of the evangelist is to sow the seed, and let the power of the word of God take root.

St. Paul writes to the Corinthians: "What then is Apollos? What is Paul? Servants through whom you came to believe, as the Lord assigned to each. I planted, Apollos watered, but God gave the growth. So neither the one who plants nor the one who waters is anything, but only God who gives the growth" (1 Corinthians 3:5–7).

The task is the same today as it was in Jesus's day. We need to lift up our heads and scatter the message of God's love generously and liberally. Archbishop Fisichella is prophetic in his words about the New Evangelization: "Still today, Jesus the evangelizer continues to call disciples to walk with him to proclaim him and the love of God. This is the challenge of the Third Millennium; a challenge which faith has always had to face and which has always found generous proclaimers."[27]

Quote

We can do no great things; only small things with great love.[28]

—Blessed Teresa of Calcutta

New Evangelization Connection

1. How is the word of God woven into the activities in your parish? How can it be incorporated more deeply into every ministry offered by the parish?
2. The sower plants in some unexpected places. Pray to the Holy Spirit to give you an opportunity to share your faith with someone whom others might consider a candidate least likely to follow Christ.

Prayer

Jesus Christ, Word of God, soften our hearts so they may be receptive to your living word. Bless those who make your word come alive through their preaching and teaching. Let us be generous in spreading your word, which brings life, especially for those who, at first glance, may seem unreceptive. Give us the confidence and joy of the sower to whom you promise a great harvest. May our prayers prepare and soften the hearts of those who don't know you so that they, too, may experience your love and eternal life. Amen.

CHAPTER ELEVEN

LUKE 10:25–37
Social Justice as Evangelization

. . .

"Which of these three, do you think, was a neighbor to the man who fell into the hands of the robbers?" He said, "The one who showed him mercy." Jesus said to him, "Go and do likewise."

. . .

There seem to be two camps in the Church today, and while we may not like to use political terms, many Catholics identify with either being conservative/orthodox or liberal/progressive. One side is characterized as being militant in obedience to the Church, and the other as being "religious secularists" who have a heart for social justice concerns but throw out the magisterium of the Church.[29]

Sometimes people who are involved with social justice ministry are perceived as being so liberal they are barely Catholic. This is an oversimplification, of course, because Catholics involved in social ministry run the gamut of liberal and conservative views, with most falling somewhere in between. Sadly, a few Catholics spend their time "bashing" the other side, when they could be putting their efforts into evangelizing the second largest denomination in America: lapsed Catholics.

Can liberals and conservatives be brought together in the work of evangelization? Is there room for those passionate about social justice issues and those passionate for dogmatic theology? The answer must be yes. All throughout his letters, St. Paul gives warnings to be alert to those who would divide the Church.[30] So how can the New Evangelization bring both groups together? The parable of the Good Samaritan provides the blueprint.

This brief, beautiful story is one of the most recognizable and popular parables that Jesus imparts. It is well known across cultures and religions, and it continues to challenge those who read it. Jesus spoke the parable in response to a dialogue between himself and a lawyer, who asked a question with the intention of testing Jesus.

The lawyer wants to know what he can *do* to inherit eternal life, as if eternal life is something we can inherit through our own efforts rather than being a gift to be received. Jesus, who is accessible and open to all questions, asks the lawyer what is written in the law. The lawyer gives a sound theological answer, and then takes it a step further and asks, "Who is my neighbor?" Jesus answers the question with a parable. By doing so, Jesus poses a different question to the lawyer and allows him to come to the conclusion himself; he gives the lawyer an opportunity to find the truth.

The parable features real places, Jerusalem and Jericho. Jerusalem sits 2,300 feet above sea level, while Jericho is 1,300 feet below sea level—a descent of 3,600 feet along the seventeen miles between the towns. With each step heading downward, the journey becomes hotter and more exhausting. Bandits, lepers and criminals were notorious for robbing the unsuspecting victim on this road, so the wise always traveled in caravans with men leading and bringing up the rear, and the women and children nestled in the middle. This formation afforded all some much-needed protection.

In the parable, a man is traveling alone on this road, and because of this, the original listeners would have judged him a fool for putting himself in such danger. So what happens next is inevitable: The man is stripped, beaten, and left half-dead. Each of these three descriptions are important details.

The fact that he was stripped shows we don't know what type of person this is: Jews, Samaritans, Greeks, and Romans each had a particular style of dress. The man's lack of clothing reveals only his humanity and leaves blank his origin. That he was beaten reveals again that he was a fool for most likely resisting the robbers; if beaten, surely blood would be present on his face and body. "Left half-dead" is a Semitic term meaning "unconscious." Were he conscious, his accent, language, or dialect could provide some clue as to who he is. Does he speak Hebrew? Greek? Instead, we are left with an anonymous human being who is totally helpless.

As the story continues we read of a certain priest who was also going down that road. Seeing the wounded man, he decides to pass by because there would be a cost for getting involved in this man's life. The priest's behavior is consistent with the laws for ritual purity and shows respect for God's law found in the Torah, which forbade coming in contact with a Gentile or a person who was bleeding. If the man had been dead and the priest had contact with him, it meant a trip back to Jerusalem for a seven-day ritual cleansing (see Numbers 19). Thus, the priest passes by the man. The Levite comes by next, and does the same thing. Finally the Samaritan sees the man and stops. The priest went past on the *other side,* the Levite went to the *place,* and the Samaritan goes to the *person.*

It is a point of intrigue in the story that the man who stops is a Samaritan. Samaritans were commonly hated by the Jews, and vice versa. Yet Jesus turns the story on the actions of this foreigner, this religious and social outcast. For the Jews, the word *good* could never be used to describe a Samaritan.

Upon seeing the man lying by the side of the road, the Samaritan springs into action. He binds up his wounds and sets him on his own animal. He binds up first, *then* offers wine and oil. This is the reverse of what one would normally do. The oil and wine soften and disinfect the wound, yet the phrase "binding up wounds" is language that is unmistakably rooted in God's saving action throughout the Old Testament. He brings him to an inn, where he takes care of the man until it is time for the Samaritan to leave. He then gives money to the innkeeper with instructions about the man's care.

After telling the story, Jesus turns to the lawyer and asks, "Who was the neighbor?" The lawyer's response is, "the one who showed him mercy." It was impossible for the lawyer to even utter the word *Samaritan*. Hearing the lawyer's response, Jesus tells him to go and do likewise: That's how to gain eternal life.

The lawyer thinks he can earn eternal life through keeping the law. By asking the question, "What must I do to inherit eternal life?" he is given a standard of behavior that does not meet his criteria. Eternal life, as it turns out, cannot be earned: It is a gift to be received. In answering the first question posed by Jesus—"What is written in the law?"—the lawyer had the correct theology: "He answered, 'You shall love the Lord your God with all your heart, and with all your soul, and with all your strength, and with all your mind; and your neighbor as yourself'" (Luke 10:26–27). Yet he could not live out the ethical standard in his daily life.

Faith in God must go hand-in-hand with compassion for all people, especially those we identify as "others." The quality of love we show to those we consider our enemies must rise to the standard set forth in this parable. Otherwise we simply love those who love us, and even the pagans do as much.

For us, then, the question is not so much "Who is my neighbor?" but "To whom must I be a neighbor?" As the parable describes in detail, regardless of language, nationality, or religion we must be neighbor to all human beings. The Samaritan, who had no doubt been a victim of Jewish hatred and vice versa, responded with a love that was an act of grace for the injured man. For the priest and Levite, strict observation of the law failed to save in and of itself because compassion exceeds the demands of the law.

In the parable of the Good Samaritan, Jesus provides a model for dealing with what anyone who evangelizes will come across: people with questions. If we let the fear that we don't have all the answers prevent us from casting our nets out, we'll never begin. In preparation, we should consider the common objections to a belief in God, to Christianity, and to our Catholic faith so that when people ask us a question we have an answer grounded in Catholic teaching. Like Jesus, the master teacher, we must remain accessible to those with differing views or those who want to justify themselves before God.

Social justice activities such as feeding the poor, providing clothes for the naked, medicine to the sick, and letter-writing campaigns to corporate and government agencies provide numerous opportunities to share our faith with others. Our direct service in meeting a person at their point of need goes hand-in-hand with the mission of Christ. We are not helping the poor and fighting for justice to earn our way into heaven, but because the mercy and compassion of Christ compel us to do so. The love that prompts us to act should also lead us to speak the name of Jesus without fear, because it is under his power, direction, and Spirit that we work for justice.

It is interesting to note that, while younger people are less active in Church today, they are more willing than previous generations to volunteer their time to social justice initiatives for those who are less fortunate. Mission trips on spring break, working in soup kitchens to feed the hungry, and collecting food and toiletries for the homeless are but a few examples of activities in which our young people and young adults get involved. In doing so, it is important to reflect: What do we model as team members? Do we socialize with the people to whom we minister, or take advantage of such activities to meet others, build relationships, and share our faith in a non-threatening ways?

All of us who are engaged in social justice ministry, no matter what our age, can process the experience in light of the parable of the Good Samaritan. Jesus said that by our love for one another people will know we are his disciples.

Love follows knowledge.[31] We should seek opportunities to deepen our knowledge of Christ, and of our Catholic faith. The goal of the Christian life is not the accumulation of knowledge, memorization of Scripture verses, or participation in liturgical rites, but to live in love, as expressed through service. No matter what form of ministry we choose, it is the place where the faith takes on flesh and blood.

Quote

You love God only as much as the neighbor you love least.[32]

—Dorothy Day

New Evangelization Connection

1. Who are the people you pass each day who are away from Mass or who no longer believe? Have you reached out to these people in any way?

2. New evangelization calls for humility in reaching out to those with whom we may have vast differences. Does your parish have any initiatives that actively reach out to those who are left on the wayside of society or who may have even been wounded by someone in the Church?

Prayer

Lord, the parable of the Good Samaritan is made real by the witness of your life. Remind us that solid theology must lead to compassionate service to others while never diverging from the truth. In putting our love for you into action may we always be mindful of the poor and those who are poor in spirit. Let us never hesitate to speak the truth of our faith, which is also an act of charity. We ask this in Jesus's name. Amen.

CHAPTER TWELVE

LUKE 15:1–7

The Seeking Shepherd: The Model for Evangelization

. . .

Now all the tax collectors and sinners were coming near to listen to him. And the Pharisees and the scribes were grumbling and saying, "This fellow welcomes sinners and eats with them."

So he told them this parable: "Which one of you, having a hundred sheep and losing one of them, does not leave the ninety-nine in the wilderness and go after the one that is lost until he finds it? When he has found it, he lays it on his shoulders and rejoices. And when he comes home, he calls together his friends and neighbors, saying to them, 'Rejoice with me, for I have found my sheep that was lost.' Just so, I tell you, there will be more joy in heaven over one sinner who repents than over ninety-nine righteous people who need no repentance."

. . .

The messenger cannot be separated from the message when proclaiming the Gospel. "Thus the Gospel is not simply about Jesus Christ, the Gospel is Jesus Christ."[33] The three parables in Luke 15, presented one right after the other, provide the method and motivation for the New Evangelization. Woven throughout each parable is the cross, the sacrifice of the one who seeks and who accepts danger and humiliation in order to restore the lost. Joy is also a key element in these parables, seen in the restoration of the lost who celebrate with family and friends.

As we examine the first parable in detail, that of the lost sheep, Jesus reveals that he not only eats with sinners, as he's accused of doing, but he actively seeks them out. Jesus models the behavior of the seekers who offer the lost a demonstration of unexpected love at great personal cost. In doing so, Jesus sets forth an example for Catholics today regarding people who are no longer in the community. What risks do we take, as individuals and as a community, to bring them back to the fold?

In the very first verse we read that the tax collectors and sinners were all "coming near to listen to him." Luke sets the stage for this parable by having it recounted to a mixed crowd: those who are religious and those who are not.

I'm convinced that the sinners drew near to Jesus for a number of reasons. First of all, they were accepted by Jesus for who they were. They had most likely witnessed firsthand how this rabbi loved and welcomed outsiders and the marginalized. Some undoubtedly had heard about Jesus secondhand and wanted to see and hear for themselves. Others may have been compelled to draw near to Jesus for reasons they couldn't explain: I call this the "holiness effect," and liken it to the holiness of God's presence manifested in the burning bush. Moses was drawn toward the bush while not understanding why; it's the same quality that people experience today when they are drawn to those who are holy.

In answer to those present who questioned Jesus about dining with sinners, he told the parable of the lost sheep. Jesus's parable is brief, beautiful, and accessible to scholar and child alike. As with most of his parables, however, a greater depth of meaning can be seen in light of Middle Eastern culture and customs.

"Which one of you, having a hundred sheep and losing one of them, does not leave the ninety-nine in the wilderness and go after the one that is lost until he finds it?" If you're like me, you've never witnessed a shepherd tending his sheep in the middle of your morning commute. When Jesus poses this question to his audience, he places it in the context of community. No one in the small villages and towns where he preached would have owned one hundred sheep. If you lived during Jesus's time you might have had five sheep, your neighbor seven, your cousin eight, and your father-in-law twelve. And no one would go out and shepherd his five sheep; the group would hire a shepherd. When we read in the Gospel, "having a hundred sheep," Jesus is speaking of the communal sheep and the shepherd is hired by the community to tend them.

Shepherds are responsible for all the sheep and as such, must have personal knowledge of them. Sheep only lie down when they are well fed and feel secure—hence the passage from Psalm 23:2: "He makes me lie down in green pastures; he leads me beside still waters." Sheep should not drink from running water because they drown easily.

A shepherd usually takes three positions while tending the sheep. First he goes in front of them to look for green pastures, fresh water, and any predators that might endanger the flock. Next he mingles among the sheep to see if any are injured or sick. Finally, the shepherd lags behind them during the trek to the pasture to encourage any stragglers to get going in the right direction. Shepherds are experts in using a slingshot, like a young King David, so they can motivate the laggards with a smack in the rear.

All of these images are familiar to the religious leaders who criticize Jesus. So when he then says about the shepherd, "and losing one of them," it is shocking to the audience. For us in the Western world it would be simply a matter of a lost sheep, but in the parable the shepherd takes responsibility for losing the sheep. Typically, a Middle Eastern man would say something like, "my sheep went from me" or "the sheep lost his way." Here Jesus places the responsibility directly on the shepherd—himself.

The shepherd in the parable is remarkable, and models the heart of God. When he realizes one of his sheep is missing, he goes after it until he finds it. And while we are impressed by the pursuing nature of the shepherd, there is more at stake here. When a sheep realizes it is separated from the flock, several things happen. First, it freezes in its tracks, shivers, makes a bleating sound, and then urinates on itself. While this is a graphic description, it highlights the desperate situation of a lost sheep. The bleating and urination send a signal to every predator in a two-mile radius that here is a free meal.

If the shepherd pursues the lost sheep, he puts himself at risk; there is no speculation involved in imagining what happens if the shepherd finds the sheep at the same time as a lion. Yet this shepherd knows the risks and goes out searching anyway. He doesn't stop seeking until he finds the sheep. Upon finding it, he puts the sheep on his shoulders because the animal is immobilized with fear, and then returns home.

The community, who may have heard that the shepherd was seeking a lost sheep, can rest assured. One sheep may not seem like much, but if you only have five sheep, then that one sheep is important. If the sheep is not found, others in the community will have to make sacrifices to make up for the one who is lost.

Jesus addressed this parable to the Pharisees and scribes, the religious leaders in the Jewish community. To whom do you relate in this story? Are you more like the sinners who drew near to Jesus, or are your actions consistent with the good shepherd? Do you question, like the scribes and Pharisees? Do you have the same fortitude the shepherd displays in venturing out into hostile territory to bring back the lost, or do you not make the effort?

The New Evangelization calls us to examine the Scriptures in light of the current state of the Church and our culture. We can close ourselves off to the world and to those who are outside the Church, or we can imitate Jesus, who seeks the lost, offering love and reconciliation, and restoring them to their rightful home. Like Jesus, we may open ourselves up to criticism from those within our community for associating with outsiders in order to bring them back. Our obedience is to God and his word, however, and not to the opinions of others.

In modeling Jesus's actions as the Good Shepherd we can become the evangelist that Christ was. We can seek those who may not even know they are lost. We can use our eyes, ears, and legs to get to the task of restoring them to our community.

Quote

For Jesus, the purpose of evangelization is drawing people into his intimate relationship with the Father and the Spirit. This is the primary reason for his preaching and miracles: to proclaim a salvation which, even though manifested through concrete acts of healing, is not meant to indicate a desire for social or cultural change but a profound experience, accessible to each person, of being loved by God and learning to recognize him in the face of a loving and merciful Father.

—The New Evangelization for the Transmission of the Christian Faith, 23

New Evangelization Connection

1. Look in your parish bulletin and consider how many programs are designed for those who are not active members of the parish. What activities or outreaches might help them draw near to the Church? How can your parish take the initiative and go to where they are?

2. Is there a mechanism in your parish community to reach out to those who are absent due to illness or apathy and let them know that they are missed?

Prayer

Lord, draw us close to your heart so your desires become our own. Let us be tireless in our efforts to be an evangelizing Church, one that attends to the lost and wounded. While attending to the ninety-nine, let us never be forgetful of those who have strayed. By our persistent prayers and invitation, may we all gather around the Eucharistic table to celebrate your love. In Jesus's name we pray. Amen.

CHAPTER THIRTEEN

LUKE 22:39–46

Prayer: Strength for the Evangelist

. . .

He came out and went, as was his custom, to the Mount of Olives; and the disciples followed him. When he reached the place, he said to them, "Pray that you may not come into the time of trial." Then he withdrew from them about a stone's throw, knelt down, and prayed, "Father, if you are willing, remove this cup from me; yet, not my will but yours be done." Then an angel from heaven appeared to him and gave him strength. In his anguish he prayed more earnestly, and his sweat became like great drops of blood falling down on the ground. When he got up from prayer, he came to the disciples and found them sleeping because of grief, and he said to them, "Why are you sleeping? Get up and pray that you may not come into the time of trial."

. . .

The process of the New Evangelization can be exciting and exhilarating. When people share the Gospel with others who then accept Christ and come back to the Church, the Word of God comes alive in their hearts once again. Then prayer is not just something they say but a deeply felt response to the person of Jesus, and a way to begin to share God's love with others.

Yet for every seed that bears fruit there are thirty, sixty, or one hundred rejections. Our enthusiasm should never waver in proclaiming Jesus, yet it is prudent to learn from Christ how he handled rejection, suffering, and the cross that lay ahead of him. For one thing is sure: We, too, will face adversity. It has been said that it's not the cross itself but how we carry it that can make all the difference to our lives. As such, it's Jesus's preparation for the cross—through prayer—that gave him the strength to carry his cross.

In the passage above, commonly referred to as the Agony in the Garden, Luke emphasizes something about Jesus's prayer that doesn't immediately come across in the text. Throughout the Bible there are passages in which parallel lines are inverted in an A-B-C-D-E-D-C-B-A structure. This is called "inverted parallelism," where the climax or main point usually appears in the middle of passage.[34] The outside verses act as a frame for the highlighted center.

Here is Luke 22:40–46 formatted to show the inverted parallelism.

A. Jesus tells the disciples to pray (22:40b)

  B. Jesus withdraws to pray (22:41a)

    C. Jesus kneels to pray (22:41b)

      D. Jesus prays (22:41c–42)

        E. Jesus is strengthened by an angel (22:43)

      D. Jesus prays more earnestly (22:44)

    C. Jesus rises from prayer (22:45a)

  B. Jesus returns from prayer (22:45b)

A. Once again, Jesus tells the disciples to pray (22:46)

We can identify the outside lines as being complementary to each other. A and A command prayer. In B, Jesus withdraws to pray and then returns from prayer in the corresponding B. Jesus kneels in prayer (C), and subsequently rises from prayer. In D, Jesus prays and prays more earnestly. This structure sets up the climax of the scene, E, in which Jesus, through his experience of prayer, is strengthened by an angel.

In this passage, Jesus leaves a lasting impression of prayer both for the disciples and for us. Prayer is not begging God to change his mind or asking for *our will* to be done, but relying on *God's will*, as Jesus does, even while asking for the cup to be removed. Ultimately, what Jesus experiences in the midst of this agony is strength for the journey.

The working document for the synod on the New Evangelization speaks of prayer and models of teaching as gifts given to the Church for carrying out the mission and task of evangelization.

> Every particular Church can boast of persons of outstanding holiness, who have been able to give renewed power and energy to the work of evangelization through their activities and, primarily, through their witness. Their example of holiness also provides prophetic and clear indications in devising new ways to live out the task of evangelization. They have repeatedly left us accounts in their writings, prayers, models and methods of teaching, spiritual journeys, journeys of initiation into the faith, works and educational institutions.[35]

Being in an atmosphere of holiness is one reason why so many people today are attracted to Eucharistic Adoration. While we may be able to explain transubstantiation and articulate that we believe Christ is present in the Blessed Sacrament, there is another factor at work that words can't express. In fact, words are not needed when we come into his presence.

I have the privilege of teaching at the Contemplative Branch of the Missionaries of Charity, Mother Teresa's sisters, in Plainfield, New Jersey. Over the years I have brought many people with me to experience evening prayer and have prayed the rosary with them in the presence of the Blessed Sacrament. Included in these groups are hundreds of high school students from varying faith backgrounds and experiences. Despite their differences, the students always comment on the remarkable, peaceful spirit present in the chapel, and how this spirit helps them to pray more deeply and effortlessly.

At any given time at the convent, there are between eight and fifteen Sisters who are in various stages of formation. I try to arrange a meet and greet with them afterward so the students can see the joy these young women possess. They have no material goods, there is not even a mirror in the house, yet they have an incredible sense of fulfillment that radiates from their faces. In an age where young people are constantly bombarded with sights and sounds from sunup to sundown, here is a place of peace, a place of holiness, a place where we can draw near to listen to the voice of God, who speaks in the silence of the heart.

We are all called to strive for holiness in order to be credible witnesses in the New Evangelization. This holiness is Christ's presence in us and in our families, which will attract and give gentle power to our words and witness. It is a quality that is desperately needed in the world today.

In the story of the Agony in the Garden, Christ the evangelist has left for us the example *par excellence* of prayer by withdrawing from the crowd, kneeling, petitioning, praying more fervently, and then rising to accept God's will for his life. The difficulties that lie ahead on the road of the New Evangelization will still be there even when we entrust them to God, but like Christ, we will be strengthened for the journey.

Quote

> May this Body immolated and this Blood sacrificed for Mankind nourish us also, that we may give our body and our blood over to suffering and pain, like Christ—not for Self, but to give harvests of peace and justice to our People.[36]
>
> —Archbishop Oscar Romero, seconds before a gunshot pierced his heart as he prepared to consecrate the Eucharist

New Evangelization Connection

1. Describe your daily prayer routine. How has your prayer life strengthened your relationship with Christ?
2. Prayer precedes and permeates the life of a disciple of Christ. Is there any aspect of being a disciple that seems to be "too much" for you?

Prayer

Heavenly Father, in Jesus's agony, he was not left abandoned but was strengthened by an angel to carry the cross that lay ahead. Strengthen us through your Holy Spirit and provide angels to help carry life's burdens when they become too difficult. We trust you in all things, knowing that you will never abandon us, for all things work together for good for those who trust you. Amen.

CHAPTER FOURTEEN

Luke 24:27–32
The Eucharist: The Heart of Evangelization

. . .

Then beginning with Moses and all the prophets, he interpreted to them the things about himself in all the scriptures.

As they came near the village to which they were going, he walked ahead as if he were going on. But they urged him strongly, saying, "Stay with us, because it is almost evening and the day is now nearly over." So he went in to stay with them. When he was at the table with them, he took bread, blessed and broke it, and gave it to them. Then their eyes were opened, and they recognized him; and he vanished from their sight. They said to each other, "Were not our hearts burning within us while he was talking to us on the road, while he was opening the scriptures to us?"

. . .

As a sports fan, I often think about sporting events at which I would have liked to have been present: a baseball game in 1926 featuring Babe Ruth and Lou Gehrig for the Yankees, playing against Ty Cobb of the Detroit Tigers; Jessie Owens and Joe Louis in the 1936 Olympics in Berlin; the game when NBA star Willis Reed limped out of the dressing room in 1969 to help the N.Y. Knicks defeat the L.A. Lakers in game seven of the finals.

Yet these events all pale in comparison to the seven-mile walk to Emmaus, and what followed afterward. What I would give to have been on that walk with Jesus and the two disciples! This was a walk to remember, not only for the two disciples but for all of us who call Jesus Lord. It reminds us that we possess the great gift of Jesus's continual presence with us in the Eucharist.

Given the circumstances of the days after Jesus's death, Jerusalem would have been the place for the two disciples to be heading. The way of Jesus goes toward Jerusalem, to the cross. In fact, there is a turning point in Luke's Gospel where we read that, "When the days drew near for him to be taken up, he set his face to go to Jerusalem" (Luke 9:51). These two disciples on the road to Emmaus are going *away* from Jerusalem, *away* from the cross. They are going the wrong way. Nevertheless, Christ meets them where they are.

What a beautiful lesson in evangelization, for Jesus does not scold or chastise the two. Instead, he takes the initiative and draws near to journey with them. The two disciples had difficulty in recognizing Jesus while walking toward Emmaus. Likewise, those who don't have the gift of faith or have not responded to the grace given them may have difficulty in seeing the face of Jesus. For those who exhibit faith, however, and trust in God, the face of Jesus can be seen in all things.

While the disciples are walking, Jesus questions them about their experience, and he listens to them as they recount their witness of his crucifixion and death. Jesus is patient as he walks and listens to facts he knows well. Our temptation might be to jump right in and tell our version of the story, but Jesus does not. Christ just listens.

Then it is Jesus's turn to speak, and his starting point is Scripture. God's truth is revealed in Scripture. Yet even after hearing God's word, the two disciples still do not understand. Their eyes are still blinded to who Jesus is. Something is missing. "When he was at table with them, he took bread, blessed and broke it, and gave it to them. Then their eyes were opened and they recognized him." They recognize Jesus in the breaking of the bread!

Their hearts burned within them while the Word of God was explained to them, yet in the Eucharist—the breaking of the bread—their eyes were opened and they recognized him. We don't really associate the Eucharist with evangelization; the emphasis is placed on sharing our personal testimony, speaking the truth in love, and solid catechesis. However, the Eucharist is foundational in evangelizing.

> The goal of evangelization today is…the transmission of the Christian faith. This task primarily concerns communities of Jesus' disciples which are organized into particular Churches, diocesan and eparchial, whose worshippers gather regularly for liturgical celebrations, hear the Word of God, celebrate the sacraments—especially the Eucharist—and look to pass on the treasure of faith to the members of their families, communities and parishes.[37]

What a beautiful connection between the recognition of Jesus present in the Eucharist and evangelization. The results of our evangelizing efforts do not end in a verbal statement of faith in Jesus, but in the full participation in the supper of the lamb, in consuming his body and blood. Even the practice of Eucharistic Adoration, as beautiful as it is, is not the final goal. St. Maximilian Kolbe said it beautifully, "The culmination of the Mass is not the consecration, but Communion."[38]

Communion with the living God, fully present in the sacrament of the altar, is the culmination and climax of all our prayer, fasting, and evangelization. Nothing less will do. For Jesus, our Passover lamb, invites us around the table of sacrifice, to receive him, body, blood, soul, and divinity, in the Eucharist. The Passover lamb is not just sacrificed, but the command from God is to partake in the Passover meal. "If Christ did not want to dismiss the Jews without food in the desert for fear that they would collapse on the way, it was to teach us that it is dangerous to try to get to heaven without the Bread of Heaven."[39]

As evangelists, we should be aware that we ourselves are often the biggest obstacle in bringing Christ to others. *My* sinfulness, *my* pride, *my* impatience, and *my* lack of love can get in the way of Christ working through me. I wish I could say with full confidence the words St. Paul said to the Galatians: "It is no longer I who live, but it is Christ who lives in me" (Galatians 2:20).

Yet God continues to use us to bring his word to the world, despite our defects. After all, it is his power working through us—not our own cleverness and intellect—that really matters. We need only turn to God in humility and prayer as a starting point for our evangelization efforts. That's why it's important for us to heed the words from the Second Vatican Council: "From the perpetuation of the sacrifice of the Cross and her communion with the body and blood of Christ in the Eucharist, the Church draws the spiritual power needed to carry out her mission. The Eucharist thus appears as both *the source* and *the summit* of all evangelization, since its goal is the communion of mankind with Christ and in him with the Father and the Holy Spirit."[40]

Pope John Paul II so firmly believed in the Blessed Sacrament as nourishment for the life and mission of the Church that he wrote an encyclical, *Ecclesia de Eucharistia*, in which he made an appeal for people to know, love, and imitate Christ. This encyclical states that "a renewed impetus in Christian living passes through the Eucharist."[41]

We need to be nourished at the altar and to bring others to Christ present in the Eucharist. St. Thomas Aquinas states it beautifully, "The Eucharist is the consummation of the whole spiritual life."[42]

In the story of the two men traveling on the road to Emmaus we can trade places with the disciples and with Christ. We who were taught the Scriptures and fed the Eucharist now have the responsibility to go forth with renewed vigor to draw near to those who have been away from Christ and his Church. We are compelled to do so.

We must bring those who no longer see God as relevant to Eucharistic Adoration and to Mass and let Christ speak to them where they are. If given the opportunity, Christ will burn within us and within the hearts of those he calls back to the Church, through the Word and of the sacrament of the Eucharist.

Quote

In his book *A New Song for the Lord,* Pope Benedict XVI speaks about the essential liturgical question, and dilemma, Catholics of our times must face. He summarizes the dilemma as this: "Jesus, yes: Church: no." In other words, many feel an attraction to Christ and may even believe in him, but they see the Church as unnecessary, and, therefore, communion with him in His Body, the Church, as unessential. However, let's take a second look at this passage [from the story of Emmaus]. As Christ vanishes from their sight, he remains. Not visible in his glorified human body, but in the humble sign of bread his own pierced hands have broken. This is how he makes himself known, is present, remains with us until the end of days.

But there is another Body in which he is known, is present within, and remains with until the end of days. The Church, the community of believers still in Jerusalem, Cleopas and his companion hoped to leave behind. Their eyes were opened to this reality as well, which is why they immediately left Emmaus and returned to Jerusalem. It is no accident that both the Church and the Eucharist have the same name, "The Body of Christ." That is why we say Jesus, yes! Church, yes!

—Msgr. Joseph G. Celano

New Evangelization Connection

1. What are some ordinary ways that we can "draw near" to those who no longer believe in God or have left the faith? How do you draw near to Jesus?

2. It may be acceptable to talk about Jesus, but speaking of the Eucharist to others is uncommon. Draw near, listen, and then invite a friend back to Mass or ask them to sit with you in Eucharistic Adoration for a short time. Over lunch ask about their experience (and pick up the bill, too).

Prayer

Lord, give us a deeper hunger for you in the Eucharist. In receiving your body and blood, let us overflow with your presence in a world that longs to be satisfied yet seeks life outside of you. Draw close to us as we draw close to those who are on roads which lead away from you. Help us to speak of your glorious death and resurrection and your desire to give eternal life and satiate our deepest longings. In Jesus's name we pray. Amen.

The Witness of St. Mark the Evangelist

CHAPTER FIFTEEN
MARK 1:16–20
Engaging People Where They Are

. . .

As Jesus passed along the Sea of Galilee, he saw Simon and his brother Andrew casting a net into the sea—for they were fishermen. And Jesus said to them, "Follow me and I will make you fish for people." And immediately they left their nets and followed him. As he went a little farther, he saw James son of Zebedee and his brother John, who were in their boat mending the nets. Immediately he called them; and they left their father Zebedee in the boat with the hired men, and followed him.

. . .

In the opening chapter of Mark's Gospel we are given a portrait of a Jesus who is very much in control, ready to accomplish the plan of salvation that God has ordained. Mark records no birth story, no genealogy, and no theological prologue. Instead, Mark begins the story of Jesus's ministry on the rocky shores of the Sea of Galilee, where fishermen are casting their nets.

The obvious place for a religious leader to begin a movement would be in Jerusalem, for the heart of religious worship took place there in the temple area. Another place you might expect a new religious movement to be launched might be the synagogue where local Jewish communities would gather to read Scripture and pray. But Jesus doesn't begin in either of these places, in the Gospel According to Mark.

Jesus is recorded as going to where the people were. In the fishing village of Capernaum, that meant the seashore. While walking along, Jesus sends a direct call to four fishermen who will ultimately help change the world.

Where do we seek potential disciples as we begin our efforts to evangelize? For the majority of Catholics, if you want to get the word out about an upcoming event you hang up a flyer or poster somewhere in the Church. Immediately you check the deadline for announcements to go into the upcoming parish bulletin, and if you want to go big, you make sure your event makes it into the diocesan newspaper.

The above approach will reach those who are already involved in parish life, who still attend Mass and grab a bulletin as they leave. The announcement in the diocesan newspaper may receive a glance from those people who actually read the paper. But if we think these meager efforts will reach lapsed Catholics and those outside the fold, we are wrong.

So how do we reach the vast numbers of people who aren't engaged with the parish? We do as Jesus did, by taking the initiative and going where the people are. This is the heart of the New Evangelization, and Catholics will need to cultivate this shift in perspective. If we are serious about reaching others and sharing the Good News of Jesus, we need to be where they are at. We should follow Jesus's lead by stepping outside of our Church circles to see the whole of our community as mission territory.

We see by the example of Jesus that evangelization begins by an intentional presence. It is a model that a few Catholic college ministries, such as FOCUS (Fellowship of Catholic University Students) and St. Paul's Outreach, are perfecting. Instead of expecting the students to come to the college chapel or the Newman Center, members of these ministries enter the cafeteria and dorms and sports fields to engage other students in conversation. It is in initiating these relationships that the foundation is laid for bringing more students into the Church. Brenda Hartner, FOCUS missionary and team director, says it beautifully. "Only by first knowing and loving an individual will you earn the right to be heard and gain the trust needed to lead them further down the road in their faith."

St. Paul told the Thessalonians: "So deeply do we care for you that we are determined to share with you not only the gospel of God but also our own selves, because you have become very dear to us" (1 Thessalonians 2:8). How often are we willing to share the details of our very lives, yet fail to open up about our faith in Jesus? We enjoy talking about a recent vacation, our children, and our favorite sports team, but when it comes to speaking about Jesus, we are at a loss.

There are reasons why Catholics traditionally don't share their faith. Historically, Catholics were discriminated against from the early days of the United States, even up through the last century. This is less true now, but the reluctance to speak up publically about our faith remains strong with some people. In addition, Catholics are more attuned to worship than to faith-sharing and, more importantly, we do not have a tradition of evangelization in our homes and in our parishes.

In your parish, how much time is allocated to reaching out to those who don't know Christ? How much time is spent outside of the parish going to meet lapsed Catholics and the unchurched? What percentage of parish finances are dedicated to reaching out beyond the parish walls to those who don't come to Church? Are pastors and parish staff members overwhelmed, in general? Absolutely! Evangelization is hard work, and requires time and effort in planning on a parish-wide basis.

Still, that doesn't negate the validity of questioning and reviewing how we spend our time and resources. Every Friday night in Texas and other southern states, Christian youth pastors are under the Friday night lights of the local football game because that's where contacts are made. The New Evangelization, when focusing on Christ, should compel us to act as Christ acted and go out to where the people are.

In living the spirit of the New Evangelization, we need to take systematic, practical steps. You can start by praying that God will give you eyes of faith to recognize and remember your call to reach out to others where they are. Can we adjust our vision to see our trips to the shopping center, sports fields, and workplace as evangelizing opportunities? Is there a non-threatening, fun event to which we would feel comfortable inviting someone who has left the Church? That may be a first step back for those who no longer worship on a regular basis. At the very least these are places where smiles and names can be exchanged and relationships formed. This strategizing is not just an individual affair; teamwork and collaboration make it much easier. Remember, Jesus sent disciples out in pairs of two.

One thing I can guarantee: When you begin to adapt a missionary and evangelizing mind-set, your prayer life will increase dramatically. You will quickly come to realize how completely we rely on God to help us in our work. God is waiting for us to act.

Quote

Never worry about numbers. Help one person at a time, and always start with the person nearest you.[43]

—Blessed Teresa of Calcutta

New Evangelization Connection

1. What events are popular in your town? How can the Church be present there through your efforts?
2. What steps can be taken to energize and mobilize the laity so they can be better missionaries in their own communities?

Prayer

Lord Jesus, you met those first disciples on the shores of the Galilee. You meet us where we are, as well. Give us the prudence to move from our prayer for those who don't believe to action on behalf of those who don't believe. Inspire our communities to be so inviting that others will experience the hope and joy we have in communion with you and the Holy Spirit. May we, as Church, venture out to a world that is desperately seeking to love and to be loved in order to present them to you, one person at a time. Amen.

CHAPTER SIXTEEN

Mark 2:1–12
Developing a Missionary Mind-Set

. . .

Then some people came, bringing to him a paralyzed man,
carried by four of them. And when they could not bring him
to Jesus because of the crowd, they removed the roof above
him; and after having dug through it, they let down the mat
on which the paralytic lay. When Jesus saw their faith, he
said to the paralytic, "Son, your sins are forgiven."

. . .

I've always been intrigued by this story. I love to enter the scene and
imagine what the day was like for those four friends of the paralytic.
I admire their selflessness because they sacrificed the possibility of
getting a good seat in the house where Jesus was teaching in order to
bring a friend to Jesus. Without saying a word or a mention of their
names, they truly incarnate and model what the New Evangelization
is all about: selfless love in action for another so that the other may
have an opportunity to know Jesus.

After the four friends hoisted the paralytic down through the roof,
I can imagine that all four looked down on the scene below from that
unique vantage point. From the perspective of the friends and the
crowd, it is likely that the physical paralysis was viewed as the man's
biggest challenge. After all, the story is focused on a paralyzed man,

not a sinful man. Yet Jesus, in his encounter with the man, takes this opportunity to show the nature and mercy of God.

Jesus's first words to the paralytic reveal God's perspective: "Son, your sins are forgiven." He addresses him as "son," revealing a familial, fatherly relationship with this man. He does not address him by his affliction but affirms the man's relationship to God by referring to him as a son. Jesus then forgives the man's sin, which of course, only God can do. As such, he is making a bold, Christological statement: that he is God.

As the story continues we learn that some of those gathered knew exactly what Jesus was saying: "Why does this fellow speak in this way? It is blasphemy! Who can forgive sins but God alone?"(Mark 2:7). Jesus takes the initiative, and says to the crowd, "Which is easier, to say to the paralytic, 'Your sins are forgiven,' or to say, 'Stand up and take your mat and walk'? But so that you may know that the Son of Man has authority on earth to forgive sins"—he said to the paralytic—"I say to you, stand up, take your mat and go to your home" (Mark 2:9–11). To the astonishment of all present, the man rises, picks up his mat, and goes home.

In evangelization, our goal is to introduce people to Jesus. This task may be made much more difficult because of a poor and inadequate introduction to Christ in the home, through the family, and through the Church.

Many people have images and ideas about Christ that are formed by the culture, and not through proper catechesis or teaching. At certain times in history, the Church and the predominant culture have used art, literature, music, theater, and other artistic forms to speak of the divine, using those outlets to reveal the beauty, majesty, and mystery of God. Too often today, however, our culture mocks Christ and casts aside his Church to the point where many people only know Jesus as he is portrayed on television.

The example of the four friends suits us well in our efforts to reintroduce Christ to those who do not acknowledge him. Their missionary mind-set, collaboration, and ability to think creatively when presented with obstacles serves as a model for us today in reaching out to others.

We must not forget the power of prayer to inspire our actions. When we look at the life of St. Paul and the lives of so many other saints we see that prayer precedes action. This action, this next step to call, to invite, to listen, and to enter into dialogue is where faith becomes exciting. It is no longer just an intellectual assent but rather engaging people whom God addresses as "son," or child, no matter how far they may have strayed.

The encounter with the paralytic takes place not in the temple, not in a synagogue, but in a home. Recall that in the previous chapter we spoke about going out to meet people where they are. How often do we view our own homes and those of others as places of evangelization? Not as a place to dictate the tenets of our faith but to model it and share it with others. In the home cited here, Jesus first forgave, then healing followed. If we want healing to take place in our homes then perhaps there is someone we need to forgive—or to ask forgiveness from.

The view from the rooftop that those four friends shared should be our view too. While they made the effort to lower their friend into the house, it is Christ who acts and remedies the problem. For Jesus, the first thing is to forgive the paralytic's sins; only then does he heal his body. How easy is it to be distracted by other incidentals in people's lives and ignore the main problem in all of our lives: sin.

Jesus is still offering forgiveness to sinners through the sacrament of reconciliation, one of his many gifts to the Church. Likewise, he continues to offer healing of our sickness and afflictions through the sacrament of the anointing of the sick. Through it all, he exceeds the expectations of those who labor at the task of creatively inviting their friends to meet Christ. Jesus continues to reach out to one person at a time.

Quote

In my experience as a preschool director, I am daily told by parents that the most important goal for their young child is to "be ready" for kindergarten. While this is true, I am always surprised at how short-sighted that goal truly is. In fact, the child will most like have a lot of living ahead (way beyond kindergarten) and what they really need is to be able to face life with the reassurance that God loves them and he will never fail them! My staff gladly teaches little ones about God's love each day in word and action! While the other skills are important, nothing in life matters more than our relationship with God. You're never too young to learn to rely and trust in him. I am so proud of the wonderful Godly women that bring the littlest ones to Jesus everyday by their loving and patient lives."

—Jeanne Polloni Bookhout, Director of
Camelback Christian School

New Evangelization Connection

1. Describe a few ways you can develop a missionary mind-set like the four friends who carried the paralytic to Jesus. What reminds you that mission territory begins right where we live?

2. The four friends knew that someone in their community needed to be healed. How does your parish share the physical and spiritual needs of its community?

Prayer

Father, all merciful and compassionate, you have created us for a relationship with you. Inspire us by the witness of love exhibited by the four friends of the paralytic. May we think of others before ourselves and use our strength and creativity to present Christ to them. We trust that your mercy, compassion, and forgiveness will heal those wounded by sin. Help us all to know that only in a relationship with Jesus Christ will we find the healing we seek. Amen.

CHAPTER SEVENTEEN

MARK 5:30–31
Evangelization on the Way

· · ·

Immediately aware that power had gone forth from him, Jesus turned about in the crowd and said, "Who touched my clothes?" And his disciples said to him, "You see the crowd pressing in on you; how can you say, 'Who touched me?'"

· · ·

In this Gospel, we read of a nameless woman whose illness would have made her and everything she touched ritually unclean. We also hear about a man named Jairus, a synagogue official, whose request was not for himself but for his beloved daughter. Jairus and the afflicted woman, two people who most likely had little if any social contact with one another, will be linked forever through their need of healing from Jesus.

This story, like many in the Gospel, reveals the depth of love, mercy, and care that Jesus shows along the way. He allows himself to be interrupted to attend to the needs of another. It also reveals that God's timing is not our timing.

Jairus asks Jesus come to his house to heal his twelve-year-old daughter. Jesus has just come back from the other side of the Sea of Galilee with his disciples, and now he is confronted by large crowds. Jairus fights through them to make his request known to Jesus; without a word, Jesus goes with him.

I can imagine the hours, days, and even weeks that Jairus must have prayed for his little girl as she and her family endured the unknown illness. I can envision him pacing back and forth while his wife dampened the little girl's head with a wet cloth as she lay on a makeshift bed on the floor. No doubt a multitude of visitors from the village came to offer prayers and advice about how to treat this illness. But nothing seemed to work. As a synagogue leader, Jairus had read the Scriptures, led prayer, and sung the psalms, but now his faith was put to the test in the midst of this crisis.

When the news reached Jairus's ears that Jesus, a teacher who had the power to heal, was in town, he went off to entreat Jesus to come to his daughter's bedside. The light of faith that may have been slowly extinguishing in Jairus's heart was lit anew as Jesus consented to come to his house. Jesus was open to the invitation, even though this account is the first record of their meeting. Jesus did not say that Jairus needed to be perfect before he would come, or that Jesus needed to interrogate him as to his level of knowledge and faith. The invitation was made and Jesus accepted.

As the crowd follows Jesus and Jairus, Mark records an incident that must have been heartbreaking to Jairus, for Jesus stopped. I can imagine the look on Jairus's face when Jesus stopped; after all, this was a life-and-death situation for Jairus's little girl, and every second mattered. Yet, Jesus stopped and asked, "Who touched me?"

What made this even more peculiar—perhaps even offensive to some—is that this woman is an outsider because of her affliction: hemorrhaging that had lasted for twelve years. According to Leviticus 15:25–30, this constant hemorrhaging would have prohibited her from full participation in the community life of Israel.

Yet Jesus stopped for her. Jesus was "immediately aware that power had gone forth from him," after the woman reached out to touch his garment. In verse 27 we are told that, "She had heard about Jesus." What had she previously heard about Jesus, and from whom? Whoever it was, that person was evangelizing and setting the stage for her encounter with Christ. The good news about Jesus was spoken by an anonymous person to this woman, and this motivated her to reach out to Christ.

How do we speak of Christ to others? We can see from this passage that someone spoke to the woman about Jesus. Someone was not afraid to share their experience and point this woman toward Jesus, which led to a miracle. How aware are we of people in our circles of influence? Are we mindful of the needs of others as we go throughout our day? Can ordinary encounters be moments of grace for those God has placed in our lives? Do we see ourselves as conduits of God's grace to a suffering world?

God's healing touch needs you and me to be the hands and lips of Jesus Christ. The graces we experience at Mass are to be brought out into the world in concrete and effective ways that can be set in motion by the realization that, like Christ, we must be aware of people around us.

Jesus listened to the woman's story as she revealed herself in the midst of a potentially hostile crowd. Jesus didn't judge her or scold her, but listened. According to Pope Benedict XVI, "By remaining silent we allow the other person to speak, to express him or herself; and we avoid being tied simply to our own words and ideas without them being adequately tested."[44]

Jesus then addresses her as "daughter," a familiar term that included her in the family of Israel, and then tells her to go in peace, which signals that she is reconnected to the community. Jesus had the courage to stop the movement of the crowd for an outsider who was desperate. It was a great moment of witness for all his disciples, to the power of evangelization and healing.

While Jesus was still speaking, a man came from Jairus's house and said, "Your daughter is dead. Why trouble the teacher any further?" (Mark 5:35). These words must have struck at the very soul of Jairus. Yet Jesus said to him, "Do not fear; only believe." In the midst of horrific news, Jesus offers hope to Jairus, and walks with him to his home.

Hope is not naive optimism that ignores the suffering of the individual and says, "all will be well." Authentic hope realizes that even though things may get worse we are confident in the fact that Christ goes with us. In his book *Salt of the Earth,* Pope Benedict XVI writes,

> To have Christian hope means to know about evil and yet to go to meet the future with confidence. The core of faith rests upon accepting being loved by God, and therefore to believe is to say Yes, not only to him, but to creation, to creatures, above all, to men, to try to see the image of God in each person and thereby to become a lover. That's not easy, but the basic Yes, the conviction that God has created men, that he stands behind them, that they aren't simply negative, gives love a reference point that enables it to ground hope on the basis of faith.[45]

In silence, Jairus follows Christ. Taking only Peter, James, and John, Jesus enters the house. When he pronounces that the child is not dead but sleeping, he is mocked, laughed at. What Jesus does next is inspiring: He throws those who are mocking him out of the house! No conferences. No sharing of feelings. No meeting to understand where they are coming from. He simply puts them out.

In our efforts to evangelize, to share Christ, to be a people of hope, we, too, will be mocked, laughed at, and outright dismissed. At those times we need to discern when to shake the dust off our feet and leave, and when to stay the course and put those who doubt out the door.

Jesus reaches out, takes the child by the hand, and speaks to her—and she got up, walked, and ate. Here was a family restored by the healing power of Jesus, who was not afraid to be touched and to have contact with those who were sick and even dead.

These two stories provide a good allegory for those who are without Christ. Evangelization is not what Jesus does, it's who he is. He is not just a person with a message; he *is* the message. Likewise, he calls his Church to be a message of hope and salvation so that the world may be alive in Christ, and experience the healing touch and new life offered to those who believe.

Both of these people in Mark's Gospel had only heard about Jesus, but somehow knew that he was their last resort. In desperation they approached and were not left disappointed. In our efforts to reach out to others, may we model Christ in our daily lives to people both inside and outside our community.

Quote

As I sit here at my godfather's bedside in the hospital, I have realized a very important "career" change; we should not be employed at our jobs, but rather be workers in life. When another human being requires special love or attention (or even if they don't), it should be our duty to be interrupted in order to comfort, love, help, and give the special attention that everyone deserves. This is the way we are able to model Jesus's miracles during our existence. Be interrupted, but let it not "interrupt" you. Instead, embrace these moments as a gift to give and receive an unexpected healing moment—the gifts of loving, giving and receiving the knowledge of love. I have received more of a benefit caring for my godfather than I believe he has received from me. His needs have taught me a different way to work by allowing me the gift of his willingness to believe in my help. You can't put a price on that.

—Dana Flynn Curto R.N., loving goddaughter

New Evangelization Connection

1. Ask God for a missionary mind-set that allows you perceive all people and interruptions as ordained by God.
2. Jesus throws out the people who are negative and are casting doubt to his word. How can you cast off doubt and be an encourager to others reflecting trust in God's word?

Prayer

Jesus, our Divine Healer, in our efforts to draw others to you, allow us to remember that evangelization often occurs when we least expect it, in the providence of our daily lives. Help us to recognize and be sensitive to those who reach out to us in small and subtle ways. May your death and resurrection give hope to all who have suffered the loss of a loved one. May we speak about you in such a way that people will desire to know more about you and inquire about the living relationship we have with you. Amen.

CHAPTER EIGHTEEN

Mark 12:29–34

Apologetics: Scripture and Catechesis in Evangelization

· · ·

When Jesus saw that he answered wisely, he said to him, "You are not far from the kingdom of God." After that no one dared to ask him any question.

· · ·

In Mark 11, Jesus enters Jerusalem to begin his passion. There he reveals his zeal for his Father's house by cleansing the temple of merchants who are using it as a marketplace. Jesus then teaches a lesson concerning a fig tree that he had previously cursed.

Figs appear at the exact same time the leaves appear on the tree, which occurs in early spring. When you see a fig tree in leaf you can also expect fruit. Jesus used this agricultural example to describe those who were outwardly religious—they had the right robes and accouterments, and the appearance of being religious—but who bore no fruit, no works of mercy. Mark makes it clear at this point that the chief priests, scribes, Herodians, Pharisees, and Sadducees are trying to entrap him.

Jesus is not afraid to go toe-to-toe with these antagonists. In fact, Jesus, who is often characterized as merely a moral teacher, is the preeminent theologian who reveals God.

In our efforts to explain and propose who Jesus is, we are going to come into conflict with others, and efforts will be made to entrap us as the religious leaders in Jerusalem did to Jesus. We know that being challenged on our beliefs is part of discipleship; we don't look for it but expect and accept it as part of following Christ. "Blessed are you when people revile you and persecute you and utter all kinds of evil against you falsely on my account. Rejoice and be glad, for your reward is great in heaven, for in the same way they persecuted the prophets who were before you" (Matthew 5:11–12).

When Jesus is questioned by people in the Gospels, it is not always meant as disrespectful—as it seems to us in the Western world. In the Middle Eastern culture, one proves his or her mettle by undergoing questioning and interrogation. We read in the Old Testament (see 1 Kings 10:1) that the Queen of Sheba questioned Solomon in order to test his wisdom. Remember that in Luke's Gospel we have a lawyer who questions Jesus about what he must do to inherit eternal life, and who is his neighbor. So while there are some in the Gospel accounts who are sincere in seeking truth, we are informed in Mark 12 that the questioning being done was not to seek Jesus's wisdom but to entrap him.

How does Jesus respond to questions and potential theological entanglements? At times, he responded with his own set of questions. Other times, he spoke in parables, or used a common image, such as a coin, as an object lesson. He invited dialogue, he challenged people's perspectives, and he used Scripture.

As we examine Jesus's interaction with people, we quickly realize that we, too, need these tools for being effective evangelists. Like the man who was blind from birth and had his eyesight restored, we can respond with a short testimony about Jesus's influence in our lives: He answered, "I do not know whether he is a sinner. One thing I do know, that though I was blind, now I see" (John 9:25).

Our personal testimony is perhaps our greatest tool in evangelization. People can argue endlessly about Scripture and philosophy in seeking to convince another that they are in the right. But presenting the testimony of your own life is difficult to argue with. St. Paul's admonition in 1 Corinthians 8:1 that "knowledge puffs up, but love builds up" should keep us grounded in the fact that we propose Christ to build up the other, not to inflate ourselves.

Just as Jesus asked questions of those who tried to entrap him, it may be sufficient to respond to our adversaries with a question or two. Jesus's first words in the Gospel of John come as a question: "What are you looking for?" (John 1:38). This is not a bad question for today as well. Throughout the four Gospels, Jesus asks close to one hundred questions. If Jesus was comfortable asking questions and allowing the listener to come to their own conclusion, then maybe we can do the same.

When being confronted about our belief in God, however, there are some who by nature are more disposed to view the existence of God through the lens of science, metaphysics, and philosophy. Therefore a philosophical or cosmological argument may not be the basis for proposing the rational belief in God and the belief that Jesus is God. The tools of science are not designed to answer philosophical questions, but the apologetic tools we need are available and are vital for transmitting the faith.

The Christian discipline of apologetics—defending our beliefs and presenting a reasonable basis for Christianity—is of vital importance for Catholics to know, understand, and be able to articulate plainly, in common language.

The common objections to Christianity and to Catholicism in particular are well known and expounded upon. "Can you prove God exists?" "Why is there suffering and evil in the world?" "Can you prove Jesus is God?" We also know that other Christian denominations will question, ridicule, and at times attack the Catholic faith with predictable questions concerning Mary, the mother of Jesus, and her role in the life of the Church; the role of the pope; the sacrament of reconciliation; justification by faith alone; and *sola Scriptura*, or Scripture alone. We need to be ready to answer these objections without anger, and in confidence.

Obviously, we can't know everything about our faith, but we should know the basics. Too often those with little or poor catechesis remain silent when asked basic questions about Jesus and the Church. We should see this as an opportunity for evangelization, and prepare ourselves accordingly. Any football or basketball coach has scouted the opposition to create a strategy to advance the ball, to take a shot. What is our strategy when someone questions the role of the pope? How do you respond when someone says that Catholics worship statues?

If we are talking about the faith to those who have drifted from the Church, sharing our story with them is a way of planting a seed and giving them something intriguing to consider. Further, we can pray for them and leave it to the Holy Spirit to move in their life.

How do we evangelize our Protestant brothers and sisters, who can be aggressive at trying to win over Catholics to their understanding of Jesus? Can we share our love of Jesus present in the Eucharist, our understanding of Scripture and tradition, and the reasons why we honor Mary? Catholics imagine that most Protestants have memorized the Bible from Genesis straight through to Revelation. This may be true in some cases, but it is not always so. And while I very much admire the love that many Protestants have for God's word and have personally benefited from their passion for and teaching of Scripture over the years, there is a difference in how we view Scripture.

Catholics believe in the importance of both sacred Scripture and sacred tradition. Sacred tradition does not refer to individual practices and customs, such as the language of the Mass, individual devotions and prayers, eating or not eating meat on Friday, and so on, but is the teaching of Jesus Christ handed on to the apostles and the Church. It carries equal weight with the Bible. Here is what *Dei Verbum* from Vatican II has to say about sacred tradition:

> Hence there exists a close connection and communication between sacred tradition and Sacred Scripture. For both of them, flowing from the same divine wellspring, in a certain way merge into a unity and tend toward the same end. For sacred Scripture is the word of God inasmuch as it is consigned to writing under the inspiration of the divine Spirit, while sacred tradition takes the word of God entrusted by Christ the Lord and the Holy Spirit to the Apostles, and hands it on to their successors in its full purity, so that led by the light of the Spirit of truth, they may in proclaiming it preserve this word of God faithfully, explain it, and make it more widely known.[46]

The Catholic Church guarantees the handing on of the word of God through the teaching authority of the pope and his bishops, who collectively are known as the *magisterium*. The magisterium ensures that no new erroneous doctrine or heresy leads the faithful astray.

We need to understand that Protestants and all those involved in denominations not in communion with the Catholic Church regard the Bible as their beginning and end. If we are to speak on a common ground with them, references to the *Catechism*, the early Church Fathers, or sacred tradition may not always be a good starting point because from their perspective "Scripture alone" is all you need.

Catholics would agree that, yes, the Bible is very important; in fact, Catholics wrote and decided what books would be included in the New Testament. The earliest piece of Christian writing, St. Paul's Letter to the Thessalonians, was written in approximately AD 51. The Gospels were not written down until thirty years or so after the resurrection, at the earliest. How did the Church exist, then, for the first twenty years or so if there was not a Bible to provide what was needed for salvation?

While I'm not aggressive at sharing the Catholic faith with Protestants, there are often occasions when someone will learn that I'm Catholic, and they begin a systematic attack of my beliefs. I'll listen and then say, "May I ask *you* some questions about Jesus and the Bible?" Most Bible-believing Protestants will jump at the opportunity because they believe that only doctrines found in Scripture are true. Most conservative Protestants and non-denominational churches believe that the Bible is all you need, but Catholics believe in both sacred Scripture and sacred tradition (see *CCC*, 74–95).

When asked where their belief in *sola Scriptura* is found, most Protestants will point to 2 Timothy 3:16 which says: "All scripture is inspired by God and is useful for teaching, for reproof, for correction, and for training in righteousness." We can agree that the Bible is a source of truth, but note that Paul said all scripture, not only scripture.

While this verse is the one quoted, they will fail to quote two verses beforehand (3:14–15), which read: "But as for you, continue in what you have learned and firmly believed, knowing from whom you learned it, and how from childhood you have known the sacred writings that are able to instruct you for salvation through faith in Christ Jesus."

The phrase "from whom you learned it" reveals clearly that Paul was referring to early sacred tradition. His phrase for "all Scripture," *pasa graphe*, means all the Old Testament books accepted by the Jews at the time he wrote his epistles. The New Testament at that time consisted only of individual books and letters; no one then was thinking of them as a single collection, and certainly not an addition to the sacred Scripture that already existed. *Pasa graphe* literally means "each Scripture," or "each passage." Paul says *all* Scripture is "profitable." His original Greek word was *ophelimos;* he did not use *hikanos*, which means "enough" or "sufficient."

In Matthew 28:19–20 we read, "Go therefore and make disciples of all nations…teaching them to obey everything that I have commanded you." In dialogue with non-Catholic Christians I ask whether Jesus intended us to teach all, or only part, of what he has commanded us. The answer is enthusiastically, all! I then read John 21:25: "But there are also many other things that Jesus did; if every one of them were written down, I suppose that the world itself could not contain the books that would be written." I then ask whether Jesus did other things not mentioned in Scripture. Was it only a few things, or a large body of teaching?

If Jesus gave us a substantial body of teaching not included in the Gospels, and intended that we teach it to the whole world, we may ask our Protestant brother or sister where he thinks those teachings are. If he does not know, we can ask him to read, 2 Thessalonians 3:6: "Now we command you, beloved, in the name of our Lord Jesus Christ, to keep away from believers who are living in idleness and not according to the tradition that they received from us." Here Paul is talking about sacred tradition. He uses the Greek word *paradises* for *tradition*. It is sacred because Paul commands it in Christ's name.

These examples are not intended to be used to beat up on Protestants but to make a scriptural defense of what Catholics believe. If we don't persuade people to our way of understanding, that's fine. We will, however, be able to articulate in a clear way why we believe what we believe. Though we have often had arguments and disagreements, my Protestant friends remain friends although we differ on some theological points.

When we don't stand firm within the magisterial teachings of the Church and begin to interpret Scripture ourselves, then we become our own pope. On my way to work each day I pass six Protestant churches. At times I have wondered why, if they all believe in *sola Scriptura*, are they so divided? Each individual congregation interprets the Bible as it suits them best, yet they all claim they interpret it correctly.

We can't know everything about the faith; the *Catechism of the Catholic Church* itself is more than nine hundred pages. But we should know some things, especially to respond to the objections from others that we know are out there. In seeking the answers to these questions we learn about the beauty and truth and rational of what and why we believe.

In the verses preceding the passage highlighted at the beginning of this chapter, Jesus has the word of God on his lips. We might dismiss this and say that Jesus *is* the Word of God so obviously he knows Scripture, but Jesus did not come out of the womb reciting Scripture. It was within the tradition of Israel that Jesus came to know the importance of God's word. This tradition started and was nourished in the home, taught in the synagogue, and lived out in the community.

Paul speaks of the word of God as the "sword of the Spirit," the only offensive weapon in the battle armor of the Christian (Ephesians 6:17). Let us hold the word of God in our hearts, treasure it as bread from heaven, and memorize it so that it will be on our lips as we proclaim Jesus.

Quote

I'm a businessman turned evangelist. My previous life was filled with annual goals, ninety-day marketing plans, and daily tasks to ensure that quotas were met. Many of my colleagues were successful in business, but complained about their families falling apart or being divorced. They had detailed plans for business, but no plan for family life. Evangelization is not about numbers, but having a plan is still necessary. I recommend that we each have a tailored approach for engaging atheists, agnostics, non-Catholics, and Catholics.

—Brian Honsberger, director of campus ministry

New Evangelization Connection

1. Investigate the Church's teachings on Mary, the pope, sacred Scripture, and other important topics and be able to defend the Church's position through Scripture.
2. Conduct or explore the opportunity to offer a Catholic apologetics course at your parish and invite someone to attend with you.

Prayer

Lord Jesus Christ, Word of God, equip us for presenting your word and the teaching of the Church to those who don't believe, or who may even be hostile to the Catholic Church. Grant us the grace to speak the truth in love. Let us not be hostile in our defense of the Church but rather be examples of faithful, intelligent, and caring Christians. Instill in us a desire to grow in faith and a longing for your word, which burns within our hearts. Amen.

The Witness of St. Mark the Evangelist

CHAPTER NINETEEN
MATTHEW 9:35–38
Motivated by Compassion

. . .

Then Jesus went about all the cities and villages, teaching in their synagogues, and proclaiming the good news of the kingdom, and curing every disease and every sickness. When he saw the crowds, he had compassion for them, because they were harassed and helpless, like sheep without a shepherd. Then he said to his disciples, "The harvest is plentiful, but the laborers are few; therefore ask the Lord of the harvest to send out laborers into his harvest."

. . .

Most people are moved with pity and compassion for those who are without food. Whenever organizations make an appeal for funds to assist those who go without food, the pictures of children with bloated stomachs, searching for scraps of food in the street or at the garbage dump, gives us pause. We feel the same compassion after a natural disaster, when homes are destroyed and peoples are killed by tornados, fires, or floods. Images of weeping families huddled together or with arms outstretched in disbelief at the damage is enough to move a person to tears.

In the passages that precede this story Jesus heals an unnamed woman who had a hemorrhage, a little girl was returned to life, two blind men had their sight restored, and a man who was mute began to speak. Jesus then saw the crowd before him, and he was moved with compassion for them. This phrase, "moved with compassion,"[47] occurs elsewhere in the Gospels, for those who need physical and spiritual healing are never far from the heart of Jesus.[48]

Are our hearts moved with compassion for those who don't know Christ as they are for those without food or shelter? If we come across a person without food or shelter, there are many things we can do to meet the immediate need; further, there are charitable organizations that can help along the way. Yet what are the options for those without the knowledge of Christ—or perhaps even more difficult, for those who have heard the message through our Catholic schools and parish catechetical programs and still have fallen away from Christ and his Church?

The modern-day apostle of common sense, G.K. Chesterton stated, "As we should be genuinely sorry for tramps and paupers who are materially homeless, so we should be sorry for those who are morally homeless, and who suffer a philosophical starvation as deadly as physical starvation."[49] Our Holy Father reminds us: "You have before you the task of seeking new ways to announce Christ in situations of rapid and often profound transformation."[50]

The message of the Gospel is the same of course, but our challenge lies in announcing the message in new ways to those who see the Church or Christ as irrelevant in today's society. On the fortieth anniversary of the issuance of *Ad Gentes*, Pope John Paul II stated: "The proclamation and witness of the Gospel are the first service that Christians can offer every person and the whole human race, as they are called to communicate to all the love of God, who manifested himself fully in the only Redeemer of the world, Jesus Christ."[51] This "first service" has at times taken a back seat to other initiatives and social programs in the Church—programs that are important but should not supersede the proclamation of the Gospel.

In Matthew 9:35, we have four keys that are helpful in expressing our compassion for those without Christ when we read that, "Jesus went about all the cities and villages, teaching in their synagogues, and proclaiming the good news of the kingdom, and curing every disease and every sickness." We can sum up these keys as such:

1. taking the initiative
2. teaching
3. proclaiming the good news
4. healing

First and foremost, Jesus took the initiative. He went to where the people were and where they gathered: in their towns, villages, and synagogues. He didn't wait for them to come to him but made the first move. "The pilgrim Church is missionary by her very nature, since it is from the mission of the Son and the mission of the Holy Spirit that she draws her origin, in accordance with the decree of God the Father."[52] We should adapt this missionary mind-set to our own lives and parishes so that we view our homes, neighborhoods, and local communities as mission fields. Jesus didn't travel to Italy or Spain to proclaim the Good News: He did it in the land of his birth.

During Jesus's public ministry he spent most of his time in and around Capernaum, as well as in Jerusalem. The distance between the two locations is approximately 120 miles. Jesus spoke the language of the people, lived life under the oppression of the Romans, ate the same food, and shared the same humor as the people of the land. Thus his parables are packed with images and experiences that were common to a Middle Eastern person in the first century AD. While some of us may romanticize about being a foreign missionary, the fact is that we are needed to bring the Gospel to our homes and to our communities, using the language, images, and technology that people today understand.

Second, we read that Jesus was "teaching in their synagogues." The title *teacher* is used of Jesus twelve times in Matthew, twelve times in Mark, sixteen times in Luke, and eight times in John. Teaching was the primary way Jesus revealed God to others. He used teaching as his vehicle for shaping ideas, forming impressions, and challenging popular belief, as well as for interpretation of the Scriptures. Jesus used teaching and education, rather than military or political power, as means by which to bring about conversion. He taught everywhere and at all times: in the temple, in the synagogues, in the home,[53] on a mountain, by the seashore, while walking on the road, while resting by a well, in places of social gatherings, during the day, and even at night.

Jesus taught through lectures and sermons, through dialogue and discussion, through stories and parables, all of which were accessible to scholar and peasant alike. The focus of Jesus's teaching was the nature of God. In the prologue to his Gospel, John states that, "No one has ever seen God. It is God the only Son, who is close to the Father's heart, who has made him known" (John 1:18). Paul writes: "He is the image of the invisible God" (Colossians 1:15).

The tasks of the teacher or catechist is to reveal Christ. In order to do this effectively, the teacher first needs to know Christ. Do we have people who are teaching about Christ who have no relationship with him? I've heard of priests looking for volunteers to teach religious education, who say, "We need volunteers for fourth grade religious ed; don't worry, you don't need to know anything, we'll give you the book." This is tragic. Imagine the fire department or rescue squad using the same mentality in looking for volunteers. You don't need to know anything—no CPR, first aid, or use of an AED (automated external defibrillator): We'll give you the book.

It is anything but compassionate to shortchange people with anything less than the truth of our faith. If we think we're doing people a favor by watering down the Gospel message or adapting the teaching of the Church to individual whims, we fool ourselves if we think that we are sensitive, humane, tolerant, or caring. Jesus gave us the truth, which is liberating.

Whether we are teaching in a classroom or informally having a conversation where questions of faith arise, we need to have both knowledge of our faith and a living, vibrant relationship with Jesus in order to give our faith away. Evangelization must permeate who we are as Church. Therefore, every activity the Church undertakes needs to be evaluated through the lens of evangelization. The apostolic exhortation *Evangelii Nuntiandi* states that evangelization includes preaching, catechesis, liturgy, the sacramental life, popular piety, and the witness of a Christian life.[54] Our evangelization and teaching must convey a person: Jesus Christ.

Third, Jesus proclaims the Gospel. Matthew closely unites the proclamation with the person and teaching of Jesus Christ: they are one and the same. The word *proclaim* is used in the Old Testament and Greek culture to speak about news of victory in battle. In the New Testament it denotes the news about God or something that concerns God. Matthew never uses it alone but in combination with teaching and the kingdom of God (see Matthew 4:23; 9:35; 24:14; 26:13). As Benedict XVI states: "The proclamation of and witness to the Gospel are the first service that Christians can render to every person and to the entire human race, called as they are to communicate to all God's love, which was fully manifested in Jesus Christ, the one Redeemer of the world."[55]

Finally, after Jesus the evangelist teaches, which feeds the intellect, and proclaims the good news, which liberates and uplifts the spirit, he heals the bodies of those who were sick. Jesus is concerned with the whole person—body, mind, and soul.

The quality of compassion is expressed in many beautiful ways through hundreds of ministries in the Church. Let us always be mindful that compassion is not limited to the temporal order or to those who suffer from ailments or poverty. Social ministry in the Church can be a powerful venue to feed the soul and uplift the spirit through proclaiming Christ's love. The New Evangelization recognizes the heroic actions and sacrifice of people who have served often quietly and behind the scenes, and seeks to introduce Christ to those whom these outreaches serve.

Reintroducing Christ to those who have left the Church through a shared concern for the poor or a service project may be an excellent place to begin anew a conversation about Jesus. In doing so, we model Jesus in his compassion.

Quote

> While we may have a natural tendency to want to "keep our faith inside" so as to not offend others, we are really hurting both ourselves and those who need to hear the truth by doing so. Keeping quiet when given the opportunity to share God's love is a great hindrance to the New Evangelization. We must

seize every chance we have to share the truth, but we must always speak with love and compassion. Hammering others about their faults and failings gets us no where. When we speak the truth in love we are allowing the Holy Spirit free range to work. Don't avoid the opportunity to tell someone about God's love. You may be the only person to ever offer such a beautiful gift to that person.

—Amber Dolle, wife, home-schooling mother

New Evangelization Connection

1. What motivates you to speak about your faith?
2. How can your parish incorporate the message of Jesus throughout the social justice ministries at your parish?

Prayer

Lord Jesus, be with those who spend their lives serving the physically poor, the disadvantaged, and those who are victims of injustice, war, and natural disasters. Bless those men and women who freely choose to share in their poverty in order to serve, as you yourself did. Move us with compassion for those who do not know you, those who seek life outside of God. Open our mouths to speak your name. Fire our hearts with zeal so that we may bring them your love and they may be nourished with your Body and Blood at the eucharistic table. Amen.

CHAPTER TWENTY

MATTHEW 10: 5–10
The "Little" Commission

...

These twelve Jesus sent out with the following instructions:
"Go nowhere among the Gentiles, and enter no town of the
Samaritans, but go rather to the lost sheep of the house of
Israel. As you go, proclaim the good news, 'The kingdom of
heaven has come near.' Cure the sick, raise the dead, cleanse
the lepers, cast out demons. You received without payment;
give without payment. Take no gold, or silver, or copper in
your belts, no bag for your journey, or two tunics, or sandals,
or a staff; for laborers deserve their food.

...

At the end of the Gospel of Matthew we have what is traditionally
called the "Great Commission" (28:19–20), in which Jesus gave his
followers the charge to make disciples, teach, and baptize in his name.
Christ assured his disciples that he would be present with the Church
as it carries out this essential mission to the ends of the earth.

Before the Great Commission was given we see Jesus giving his
disciples a small or "limited" commission, in which they were sent
forth. In Greek, the word for "one who is sent forth" is *apostolos*, which
is translated as "apostle," and they were endowed with the authority
of Jesus. Jesus instructs them at length before he sends them out on

mission, and he warns them of impending danger as well as of the sacrifice and rewards that await them.

It is important to consider that Jesus limited their scope of evangelization strictly to the house of Israel. He forbade them to enter pagan territory or any Samaritan town in the Galilean countryside. This limitation allowed the twelve to specialize and concentrate on a particular area and a particular type of person in their evangelization efforts. The mission was clear: They were to prepare the Jewish people for Jesus.

This type of specialization in evangelizing can be clearly seen on the life of the early Church, where St. Peter focused on bringing the good news of Jesus to the Jews, or circumcised ones, while St. Paul focused on the Gentiles—those who were uncircumcised (Galatians 2:7–9). Paul would give more precision to his mission by stating that he would focus on spreading the Gospel of Jesus where others had not yet gone (Romans 15:20).

This specificity in defining the mission makes evangelization much more manageable. If you have a clearly stated mission to evangelize college students or mothers of preschool children or those who work in the medical profession, then these are the people who should be your primary concern. We can easily become overwhelmed and burned out in ministry because our focus is undefined or too broad. Jesus focused on certain groups in his ministry and teaching, and that is what Peter and Paul did, and what we must do as well if we are to be successful in our efforts.

Too often, we who minister in the Church want to be all things to all people, but we end up accomplishing very little and burning out. While it's sometimes difficult to concretize our results, there are benchmarks that help us see if we're being effective. For example, if the same two people show up to a youth group or men's group meeting after six months, then we probably haven't done all we can to attract new members.

Let's evaluate this by business standards: If after six months you had only two clients or made only two sales, most likely you would be fired. Yet in the Church, a person can go on and on without achieving recognizable results. One priest described a poorly run youth ministry program in his parish this way: "It was like the body was on the slab at the mortuary but nobody had the guts to declare it dead."

When we specialize in who we are trying to reach we can match gifts, talents, and desires to a particular audience. For me, reaching out to those who are involved in sports is natural because I like and play sports. The best people to reach out to businesspeople are not priests and bishops, but other businesspeople. It's a natural fit. The unique skills, background, and interests each of us possess make evangelization easy because they provide a natural flow of conversation when reaching out to people of similar backgrounds. Paul makes it clear that the body of Christ, the Church, has different functions. Our efforts are most productive when we focus on people with whom we have a natural fit.

Father Thomas A. Judge, who lived in the early 1900s, understood this idea of like-to-like, indigenous evangelization. He questioned why so few African Americans responded to the evangelization efforts of the Church, and when asked to send missionaries to the South from the North his answer was an unequivocal "no." Rather than a ministry from outside the region, he proposed that the evangelization of black people must come from themselves. He recommended that possibly six religious sisters could train thirty or fifty young African American women in the Cenacle methods. These women, then, would work in "'missionary neighborhoods." The Cenacle "would supervise," but the principal missionary work would come from within the African American community."[56]

Most priests expect that being available to all who come and ask of their time is part of their vocation. Time, of course, is limited and we should not expect the priest to be the one to head up every outreach effort. Some people are suited for engaging large groups, while others are better one-on-one; each has their own gifts.

As a Church community, how can we assist the priest or pastor in reaching out to those within the parish, especially those who do not practice the faith? According to canon law, the pastor, "With the collaboration of the faithful...is to make every effort to bring the gospel message to those also who have given up religious practice or who do not profess the true faith."[57]

Many pastors would love to have the participation of all the Catholic faithful who are registered in the parish, yet we all know that many who are registered in a parish don't actively participate on a regular basis. This is precisely why we need to assist our clergy in the New Evangelization.

As a parish community, the starting point for evangelization is prayer followed by an executable plan of action. What are the characteristics of the parish community? Ethnicity, location, affluence, education, and parish history are all elements to be considered in evangelizing efforts. But beware of prepackaged, one-size-fits-all programs. What works for a rural community in Alabama may not work in an industrialized city in New Jersey. Each community has its own set of circumstances and its own flavor. Consider how Jesus used different images and teaching styles to communicate his message. Jesus knew his audience was both in the rural area of Galilee, where people were generally less educated and even looked down upon by the literate, and among the well-schooled religious leadership of Jerusalem. God's love is for all, yet how Jesus communicates the message is different for each group.

In Galilee, Jesus uses parables more frequently and employs common images from everyday life to carry the truth about the kingdom of God. The mustard seed, leaven, a net, a pearl, a lost sheep, the sower and the seed, garments, and wineskins were all familiar to the rural Galilean. In the parable about the barren fig tree in Luke 13:6–9, we see the introduction of the word *manure*. This would be abhorrent to the city-dweller yet seen as a vital component to the rural farmer. For those who were fluent in the law, like the scribes and Pharisees in Jerusalem, Jesus spoke about the law and quoted verses from Scripture.

In our own efforts to evangelize we should look at our gifts, talents, and interests and look around to see who are in our social or peer group may be in need of hearing the good news. While we should never turn someone away who inquires about our belief in Christ or refuse to share our story, it is best to begin with the people we are comfortable with.

Of course, this presumes we have a story to communicate. For Catholics, sharing our faith may not be something we are proficient in—for a number of reasons. In our practice, we focus more on worship than on sharing the faith. Also, most of us rarely have witnessed someone Catholic sharing their faith: This might seem "too Protestant" to us. Finally, when Catholics came to America, they were a minority and were persecuted and discriminated against. So we learned to keep our faith to ourselves and witness to our faith by living a good life.

Most people are comfortable sharing stories about the people and things that are important to them: family, grandkids, a favorite vacation, restaurant, or sports team. We can go on and on about these topics with ease and freedom. Yet when it comes to sharing our faith, we are more often than not left speechless. We may talk generically about our parish or about God in general, but too often fail to speak about our relationship with Jesus. This is a roadblock that must be overcome: A Catholic culture where one does not speak about Jesus Christ needs to change.

One outline you can use for developing your own story of faith begins before you encountered Jesus, moves through the experience of committing to a relationship with Christ, then notes how your life has changed since committing to that relationship. You should develop a brief, three-minute witness story. Don't get sidetracked with the particulars, just state plainly the facts about your life.

Perhaps as a child you went to church on Sunday and Catholic school during the week, yet you were never really at peace with yourself and God. Then as a young adult, through a retreat, a person, a prayer service, whatever, you invited Christ to be Lord of your life. Since then you pray regularly, attend Mass faithfully, and as the Word of God comes alive in your life, you start to see God's hand in a real, tangible way. This has affected your life in a concrete way. If you can say something like this enthusiastically and with a heartfelt smile, you're on your way.

What Jesus asked his disciples to do was to make a proclamation that the kingdom of God is at hand. As we go along our way with the various activities of our lives, we too should have a proclamation—the good news of Jesus Christ. We should be able to proclaim Christ and his Word, which has the power to save.

With every commission there are pitfalls to avoid. We want to focus on Christ rather than be entertaining, and ask ourselves questions such as these. Are we asking people to consider Christ and grow in Christ, or are we just looking for Church membership? Do we allow ourselves to become sidetracked by politics and non-essential issues in our discussions with the unchurched?

Do we know at least some Church teaching and Scripture that we can offer as responses to those who may have objections to the Catholic Church? Do we have an eye for those who are lost, for the ones who appear to have it all but who, without Christ, are dying inside? Do we reach out to those who may have been hurt by the Church and listen to their stories in hope of reconnecting them with the Church? Does evangelization permeate everything we do as a parish so that evangelization becomes who we are as Catholics?

In the "little" commission, the focus is on building the kingdom of heaven in the vicinity of Jerusalem. Jesus later will expand this commission to include bring the Gospel Christ to all nations. We read in the Acts of the Apostles that Philip went to Samaria to preach; most notably, Paul will take the Gospel west, to the region of Galatia, to Ephesus, to Corinth, and ultimately to Rome.

Like these early evangelists, we can begin to reignite the fire of faith that the Holy Spirit stirs within and make a difference in this world for Christ.

Quote

Go headfirst and wholehearted down the path of what you believe in; it is hand-painted by God to lead to greatness. For him, nothing is impossible. Therefore, never fear where he guides your heart and always do what you love. It's what the world expects of you.

—Meghan Brulé, ballet dancer

New Evangelization Connection

1. What groups would you naturally fall into (e.g., businessperson, grandparent, stay-at-home mom, single person)? How can your parish offer an event for people in one of these categories who may not be regular churchgoers?

2. How can parishes within a diocese help serve the needs of parishioners without having to reinvent the wheel at each parish? Can neighboring parishes assist each other in identifying and reaching out to specific groups?

Prayer

Lord God, often those who desire to serve you just don't know where to begin. Sharpen our focus and limit our scope to the people you want us to reach out to. Allow us to serve you in little ways lest we become overwhelmed. Help us to use our time and resources wisely in our ministry, and put a particular group of people on our heart so we may begin to reach out and invite them to a relationship with your son. In Jesus's name we pray. Amen.

MATTHEW 11:28–30
The Invitation of Jesus the Evangelist

. . .

Come to me, all you that are weary and are carrying heavy
burdens, and I will give you rest. Take my yoke upon you,
and learn from me; for I am gentle and humble in heart, and
you will find rest for your souls. For my yoke is easy, and my
burden is light.

. . .

Fulton J. Sheen is famous for having said, "There are not a hundred
people in America who hate the Catholic Church. There are millions
of people who hate what they wrongly believe to be the Catholic
Church—which is, of course, quite a different thing."[58] The same can
be said about Jesus and his teaching.

How often have I heard someone say, "It says somewhere in the
Bible that…" when in fact, nowhere in the Bible does it say what the
person implies. Thank God for the Catholic Church in preserving
the Word of God and for the early Church Fathers and councils in
the first centuries of the Church who, guided by the Holy Spirit, gave
us the New Testament we have today.[59] We are fortunate to have the
word of God proclaimed at every Mass. Because Catholics follow a
three-year cycle of Scripture readings at Mass, a Catholic who attends
liturgy every day or follows the daily readings at home will, over the
course of those three years, hear almost all of the Bible read.

In the Old Testament the prophets issued an invitation to Israel: turn to God, repent, and seek the Lord. In the New Testament Jesus invites people to come to him, Emmanuel, God incarnate. Each of these invitations is given in love. Love never forces its will upon another; this would be against the very nature of divine love. It comes as an invitation, a gift to be received and not a puzzle to be solved.

When Jesus speaks about "all you that are weary and are carrying heavy burdens," one of the burdens he is referring to is the law and its obligations, which one must live out as a faithful Jew. Understanding that our sin separates us from God is another burden that we must bear, and it can certainly weigh us down. When we lay down our burden, what follows is the promise of rest. For the Jewish listeners *rest* is closely associated with the Sabbath, where one rests from earthly duties and celebrates with their family. Jesus offers rest through obedience to his word. Freedom from the guilt of sin and its side effects of anxiety, fear, depression, and doubt are done away with and replaced with Christ himself, who is love, joy, and peace.

For those who have heard of Jesus and the Catholic Church yet identify themselves as nonbelievers or unaffiliated, what would they say to the invitation of the Church to lay their burdens on the shoulders of the Lord? Are they even aware that there is such an invitation? What message do we give these people through our words and action? It is a challenging question, for sure. Do we emphasize those things which are not essential to the faith? Do we see ourselves like the older brother in the parable of the Prodigal Son, as a servant rather than a beloved child of God? Do we see ourselves like the Father, humbly entreating his sons to come to the table?

Before we focus on reaching out to those who may be apathetic to the Church, how well do we retain the people we have? When we understand that God continues his invitation through us, his Church, it might give us pause to reflect on how we welcome those who already attend.

In the business world it is commonly said that it takes much more work to win back an existing customer who has left due to a bad experience than to retain current customers and make sure they are cared for. In talking to those who have left the Church, I have never met a person who has left because of theology and what the Church teaches. Most often they leave because of something someone on the parish staff did to cause them to leave. This is indefensible.

They leave because they've been insulted or ignored by the priest, parish secretary, or director of religious education. They can trust the teaching of the Church, but they refuse to be treated unjustly. I understand that there are two sides to every story, and that some parishioners make unrealistic demands on priests and parish staff. But usually the unrealistically demanding people are the ones who stay!

Recently my mother, a faithful Catholic for all her life, was at a party for a friend, and the pastor of her parish showed up. When my mother said hello, she mentioned that she had been a member of the parish for over forty years. To that the pastor responded, "Oh, you're one of those old ladies who sit in the back." My mother was hurt by this comment, and rightfully so.

What a difference it would have made if this pastor had said something like, "Wow, over forty years in the parish! Thanks for your faithfulness and commitment to the Church. You've witnessed a great deal of change in the Church during your lifetime and have remained faithful through it all. Thank you. It means a lot to me as pastor to see you each week." It would have taken no more than eight seconds to say something like this. What a shame: It would have taken just a few minutes to gain some wisdom from this woman of faith, a true disciple of Jesus who has remained faithful to the Church.

As evangelists, we need to model evangelization so our parishioners can catch a glimpse of the zeal and excitement we have for Christ. We need to encourage them, listen to them, and show them how they are a part of the mission of New Evangelization. Invitations need to be made continually and creatively.

There is an old marketing adage that states a customer needs to see or hear your message seven times before responding. In our current culture people are constantly bombarded with messages, and it is difficult to get the message out there. Different approaches are needed for different age groups and personalities. How do you get the Catholic message out in the public arena? How well does your parish announce the good news and the activity of the parish to non-Catholics?

Many people think that they don't need Jesus or a parish. They may be doing just fine without them, at least for now. Yet there are times of need in people's lives when we can and should make the effort to be present. We just need to look at the local paper to see who's been in a accident, who's welcoming a new baby, and who just moved into our neighborhood. Are we ready to stop by and greet them or offer words of hope, welcome, and comfort?

Americans like to be invited to events—not groups. Groups seem to entail a commitment, and most Americans are skeptical of people who want a commitment right away. We are very possessive of our time. But although there is a cost to following Jesus, Christ assures us twice in the passage from Matthew that he desires to give us rest from our burdens. That is a message that can resonate in the hearts of people.

Often the real issue at hand is trust. When I hear of a great bargain or receive a mailing that promises a once-in-a-lifetime offer, I ignore it and toss it in the trash. Who are these people who want to give me something for nothing? But when a deal is introduced by someone I know and trust, my perspective is different and I at least give a listen. The difference is not always in what the message is but in who's delivering it.

When we ask someone to consider coming back to the Church or entering into a personal relationship with Jesus, we need to remember that this invitation comes through the Church. Vatican II teaches that the Church is the "sacrament of salvation."[60] Jesus intended that the Church be a sacrament of the inner union of all people with God. This means that the Church is an effective sign of salvation for all. Jesus accomplishes his saving work in and through the Church, then through you and me. So we need to be a community whose mind-set is one of constantly inviting and reaching out to those who are in the Church, empowering them to go out to invite others.

At one of the big retail stores near my home there is always a greeter at the door who gives me a big hello and a smile when I go in. When I see companies and retailers doing little things like that to ensure the well-being of the customer, it reminds me that I'm doing those things for a much greater cause, namely the Gospel. What would it take to have a welcoming entrance at the doors of your parish? Even more importantly, at the doors of the Church itself?

Let's start by inviting others to follow and fall in love with Christ.

Quote

What we need most in order to make progress is to be silent
before this great God with our appetite and with our tongue,
for the language he best hears is silent love.[61]

—St. John of the Cross

New Evangelization Connection

1. While people may be wary of entering a group, they are usually
   open to being invited to an event where issues of faith may be
   brought up. What event could be held, either at your church or at
   a neutral site, that would be attractive to those who are away from
   the Church?

2. Jesus invites us to come to him. Does every event that goes on
   in the Church, from religious ed to distributing food at the food
   pantry, have an evangelizing element to it?

Prayer

Lord Jesus, we who have accepted your invitation to follow you know
the joy and peace that come with discipleship. We know too, that in
carrying our burdens, you assist us along the way, coming to our aid.
Help us find the right words of invitation for those who have been
away from the Church or who may not know of your love. May we be
people who point to you as the Way, the Truth, and the Life. Amen.

CHAPTER TWENTY-TWO

MATTHEW 28:16–20
The Great Commission

. . .

Now the eleven disciples went to Galilee, to the mountain to which Jesus had directed them. When they saw him, they worshiped him; but some doubted. And Jesus came and said to them, "All authority in heaven and on earth has been given to me. Go therefore and make disciples of all nations, baptizing them in the name of the Father and of the Son and of the Holy Spirit, and teaching them to obey everything that I have commanded you. And remember, I am with you always, to the end of the age."

. . .

There are moments in our lives when we prepare ourselves for the inevitable partings in life. Graduating college, moving out in different directions from our friends, seeing a spouse off for a tour of military duty, and being at the bedside of a loved one who is dying are but a few examples of times when we learn to say good-bye.

The eleven disciples have been through a great deal in their three-year journey with Jesus. During the time of his passion, death, and resurrection they experienced an entire range of thoughts and emotions—from denial, betrayal, fear, disbelief, cowardice, horror, and depression to euphoria, astonishment, forgiveness, love, and unbounded joy.

In the last act of the Gospel of Matthew, Jesus prepares his disciples for his own departure and gives them a commission that will change the world and turn it upside down. It is a commission that continues today through his Church. I wonder who spoke first after Jesus ascended to heaven? I wonder what was said as these men got up off their knees and realized the task that lay ahead: implementing the first wave of evangelization.

Even during Jesus's lifetime the disciples were faithful in carrying out what is commonly called the "Great Commission." They were the ones who were chosen by Jesus, traveled with him, and had the responsibility to make disciples, baptize, and teach people. Their example was Christ, of course, but did he leave behind an executable blueprint? Was there a planning meeting to decide where to start and how to go about implementing this mission that included "all nations"? Quite a task lay ahead of these first disciples. How would they communicate God's love and plan of salvation into distant lands and foreign cultures?

There are a few lessons we can take from the disciples as we embark on our own efforts of evangelization. Before going out, the first disciples committed themselves to prayer, fellowship, and the breaking of bread; so must we. We are responsible for the depth of our relationship with God, while God is responsible for the breadth of our outreach. Because the Holy Spirit is the director of all evangelization, we need to be attentive to the promptings and movement of the Spirit.

Jesus assures the disciples: "All authority in heaven and on earth has been given to [me]." Jesus, on the basis of his authority, is very specific as to what the disciples are to do; "Go, therefore, and make disciples of all nations, baptizing them in the name of the Father, and of the Son, and of the Holy Spirit, and teaching them to obey everything that I have commanded you." The call to go out to all nations recalls the faith of Abraham and his wife Sarah, who were called by God to go from their land (Genesis 12:1–9). This call meant more than simply entering the land and winning a few converts for God, but rather, changing the very fabric of society in order to prepare for Christ.

Jesus's commission is followed by words of encouragement: "I am with you always." Jesus is with us as a Church, and through his eucharistic presence as we proclaim the Gospel (Matthew 18:20; 26:26–28, CCC, 860, 2743). His promise to be with us is similar to the promise God gave to Moses (in Exodus 3:11–12), to Joshua (1:5), and to the nation of Israel (Isaiah 41:10). This promise provides comfort in times of trial and distress. With these words of encouragement all disciples can come down from the mountain and go out into the world.

The actions taken by those first disciples wasn't frenetic, undisciplined, or random. As Augustine would write three hundred fifty years later, "Peace is the tranquility of order."[62] Peter and Paul were specific in their outreach, to the circumcised and uncircumcised, and the other disciples had their specific mission areas as well. In proclaiming the Gospel to foreign lands and in divergent cultures, they knew they had to read the "signs of the times." Even down through the ages to today, this phrase appears in the introductory statement *Gaudium et Spes:*

> To carry out such a task, the Church has always had the duty of scrutinizing the signs of the times and of interpreting them in the light of the Gospel. Thus, in language intelligible to each generation, she can respond to the perennial questions which men ask about this present life and the life to come,

and about the relationship of the one to the other. We must therefore recognize and understand the world in which we live, its explanations, its longings, and its often dramatic characteristics.[63]

The desire and ability to read the signs of the times is something very much in the forefront of the Catholic Church. The Synod on the New Evangelization for the Transmission of the Christian Faith, which took place in October 2012, reflects the movement of the Holy Spirit in the Church. Realizing that she must always be a student of society and of culture in order to present the Gospel of Jesus Christ in a clear authoritative manner, the Church sought to present this outreach in practical and inspired ways.

In the *Lineamenta*, the planning document in preparation for the synod, Pope Benedict XVI, cautions,

> The missionary mandate which concludes the Gospel (Mk 16:15ff; Mt 28:19ff; Lk 24:48ff; Acts 1:8) is far from being fully carried out; it has simply entered a new phase.... The Churches in traditionally Christian countries, for example, involved as they are in the challenging task of new evangelization, are coming to understand more clearly that they cannot be missionaries to non-Christians in other countries and continents, unless they are seriously concerned about the non-Christians at home. Hence missionary activity *ad intra* is a credible sign and a stimulus for missionary activity *ad extra*, and vice versa.[64]

Being Christian and "being Church" means being missionary in nature. Loving one's faith implies bearing witness to it, bringing it to others, and allowing others to participate in it. A lack of missionary zeal is a lack of zeal for the faith. Our faith is made stronger by transmitting it. The pope's words on the New Evangelization can be translated into a rather direct and crucial question: Are we interested in transmitting the faith and bringing non-Christians to the faith? "Are we truly missionary at heart?"[65] He concludes by saying, "Today, a 'business as usual' attitude can no longer be the case."

We must develop opportunities for implementing the New Evangelization strategies, and investigate new ways of approaching the culture. St. Francis de Sales reminds us: "Great occasions for serving God come seldom, but little ones surround us daily; and our Lord Himself has told us that 'he that is faithful in that which is least is faithful also in much.'"[66] In our desire to do great things we should remember that little opportunities surround us.

In the New Evangelization, we are called to reach out to those who have left the Church, are apathetic, feel they don't need God, or don't want to bother with any of the demands God may make on them. Jesus has given us our mission statement: We don't need to spend time figuring out a new one. What we do need is an evangelization plan for each parish. We need to read the signs in our own diocese, parish, and communities, and after prayer and discernment, begin to implement our plan with joy and hope.

In assessing the character of our parish and community we can begin to identify our strengths and weaknesses by reaching out to our neighbors through the lens of the New Evangelization. There will be bumps along the way, and mistakes will inevitably be made but progress will take place as well. Mother Teresa reminds us that we are called to be faithful, not successful.

Jesus first gave the disciples their "little" commission, focused specifically on the Jewish towns and villages they knew well. The master evangelist was preparing them and the Church for this new movement of the Spirit, this Great Commission to undertake anew the Church's fundamental mission. The means by which individual communities will express the proclamation of the kingdom of God begun in Christ will be unique for each community, because each faces different challenges and opportunities. Every Church and every ecclesial movement, be they active or contemplative, religious or lay, must evaluate what they are doing in light of Christ's call to proclaim the Gospel.

The Church today calls us to a continuation of the Great Commission. "Go therefore and make disciples of all nations." Convert all hearts to Christ, "baptizing them in the name of the Father and of the Son and of the Holy Spirit." Gather the converted into communion,[67] "teaching them to obey everything that I have commanded you." Ensure proper catechesis.

Teaching about Christ is not merely the conveyance of facts from one person to another. In this sense, for the New Evangelization, teaching can be more associated with the Latin word *tradition*, which communicates the idea of handing over or giving up something with the intention of passing ownership to another. We are entrusted with passing on the teaching of Jesus and communicating the person of Jesus—not just facts about the faith.

The New Evangelization must not be reduced or relegated to the work of one group within the Church: It belongs to all of us who are Church. The great commission calls every baptized Catholic to become a person who can speak with freedom and joy about Jesus.

Quote

As I stated in my first Encyclical *Deus Caritas Est*: "Being Christian is not the result of an ethical choice or a lofty idea, but the encounter with an event, a person, which gives life a new horizon and a decisive direction" (n.1) Likewise, at the root of all evangelization lies not a human plan of expansion, but rather the desire to share the inestimable gift that God has wished to give us, making us sharers in his own life."[68]

—Pope Benedict XVI, *Ubicumque et Semper*

New Evangelization Connection

1. To go out and make disciples is a direct call from Jesus. What types of discipleship groups are available in your parish? Are there people who can disciple and mentor others one on one?
2. Teaching, or catechesis, is essential to passing on the faith. Do the catechists in you parish teach in such a way that their message communicates the person of Jesus along with Church teaching?

Prayer

My Lord and my God, when the task of bringing the message of your love and forgiveness to the world seems overwhelming, encourage our hearts with your Holy Spirit. Remind us that the Gospel is spread one person at a time and that no word spoken out of love for you is ever wasted. We pray for our Holy Father, the bishops, priests, deacons, and laity, that they will be faithful witnesses to the Gospel and lead in the area of the New Evangelization. In Jesus's name we pray. Amen.

PART SIX

Moving the Church From a Maintenance Mind-Set to One of Mission

If the New Evangelization mind-set is to truly take root in us, then we must be prepared to accept a change in the Catholic culture. The Catholic Church has a definite structure and hierarchy, and the many outstanding pastors, bishops, and cardinals who model leadership through their words and actions offer an invaluable gift to the Church. In the New Evangelization, however, leadership from the hierarchy and synod exhortations alone will not be sufficient if the laity are not willing to step out in faith and reach those who have left the Church.

The structure of the Catholic Church provides oversight for the enormous organizational task of leading over 1.3 billion Catholics worldwide. And though the leadership of the Church is admirable in many ways, there are always limitations when dealing with an institution of this size. A friend once told me that he didn't believe in "organized religion," to which I replied, "Join the Catholic Church. We're not that organized!" While I made that comment in jest, there is some truth to the statement.

We can always point to churches in any diocese across the United States that are model parishes, yet there are still numerous dioceses and parishes that struggle. The model parishes often have financial resources and trained personnel to run numerous ministries, as well as a pastor who has a vision, works well with others, and delegates responsibilities.

Other parishes aren't so lucky. Often we find that Catholics in struggling communities are sacramentalized but not properly catechized or evangelized. While there are many reasons for this— lack of resources, overworked priests, no clear vision for the parish, disinterested parishioners—these problems must be addressed. We need to see parishes change from simply trying to make it through next Sunday to being places where a vision has been established and evangelization is woven into the fabric of the parish.

When implementing the New Evangelization is solely the responsibility of a committee rather than the responsibility of every Catholic in the pew, it signals the beginning of the end for evangelization in that parish. When a missionary mind-set is not woven through every program and event in the Church, but instead lies in the domain of a few and not all, parishioners will not take ownership and will view evangelization as the responsibility of others.

Changing the Culture of a Parish

But there is hope! Just as we find great diversity within parishes across the nation there is great diversity in how we implement evangelization initiatives. There is not a set program for a parish to follow; rather, each diocese and parish is asked to identify their own particular culture so that they can begin to pray, dialogue, and take steps to train parishioners to evangelize first within the parish boundaries.

The culture of a particular parish can change when leadership is viewed as a collective activity between the pastor and parishioners. A good starting point is establishing a means of listening to one another, learning together, and discussing how best to bring the Gospel to those who have drifted away from the Church.

Motivating faithful churchgoers to be evangelists is a challenge as well. Leadership from within the community will often emerge based on the expertise of parishioners and the vision for the parish community. If the pastor is not willing to use resources to reach out and evangelize, the parish will most likely become a sacrament distribution center where no new disciples are formed and growth is stifled.

As the Church faces change within the secular society, we need to invest intentionally in a leadership culture that will match the unfolding challenge. The beliefs that drive leadership behaviors need to align with the operational evangelization strategy, which will differ according to the parish demographics and needs. We must take advantage of the great leadership in the larger Church—including Pope Benedict XVI and many courageous U.S. bishops—who are moving us forward with a renewed vigor to return to our evangelizing roots.

This changing landscape requires not just new skills or prepackaged programs, but a new mind-set that makes evangelization the responsibility of every baptized Catholic. Hidden assumptions may be unearthed through dialogue between parishioners and the parish staff. Years of status, authority, and control by one person or a particular group in the parish may have led to behaviors that are archaic, unnecessary, and at odds with where the Church needs to move: These, too, will need to be addressed and dealt with.

Pastors and priests from foreign countries may have a view that is different from American Catholics about what it means to be Church. When they act out of good intentions yet fail to include parishioners in decision-making or discussions, disaster will likely follow. Anger and resentment sets in, causing dissension, division, and "hot" letters to the local bishop. Most American Catholics want to be included in decisions that will affect them and their families. When the parishioners and their opinions are valued, change can occur swiftly.

A year ago I was helping my three young daughters make a smoothie while my wife was out. The supplies were ready: fruit, milk, yogurt, and juice. When I turned my head for a split second, someone hit the "blend" button before the top was on. The results were spectacular! Fruit, milk, yogurt, and juice went flying in all directions. As my children looked at my face for a reaction, I momentarily froze and then said, "That was awesome!"

The three seconds of chaos then led to thirty minutes of cleanup before my wife arrived home. Somehow, her standard of clean and mine differ, and she quickly pointed out areas that I had missed. But there was one area that we both missed until the next day. The silverware drawer had been flooded and the wood on both sides had begun to warp. My wife moved the silverware to another drawer, and then waited a week for me to replace the wood in the warped one. After I replaced the wood, she decided that she liked the new silverware location better and it remains there to this day.

Why am I sharing this tale of woe? Well, it's been over a year since the blender incident occurred, but at least once a week I reach for a fork or knife in the drawer where they were previously located. It's a reminder to me that change is difficult, and it is so easy to revert to the old way of doing things. Johnny Cash once told a young reporter who criticized his simple style of playing guitar, "Kid, if it was easy, everybody would be doing it." We need to constantly communicate what evangelization is, repeating and reinforcing it often, and then saying it again, to the parishioners and staff.

Practical Steps for Evaluating and Implementing Parish Programs for the New Evangelization

While evaluating parish programs in light of the New Evangelization, it is critical to have the parish community and those in key positions get together and discuss what evangelization is. Parish council members, directors of religious education, catechists, music ministers, liturgy specialists, and secretaries should have the opportunity to learn what evangelization entails, then discuss it and ask questions so that everyone is on the same page. Make a commitment to *sentire cum ecclesia*, or "think with the Church" in this endeavor.

A good first step is to compile a list of every ministry the parish has to offer, from the Holy Name Society to the finance council. Start with a few broad questions about the ministry itself, specifically related to evangelization. Are the activities of the group faithful to Scripture and the tradition of the Church?[69] Is it helping others grow in their faith through Scripture, prayer, service, or the sacraments? Is it bringing people together in the spirit of communion or fellowship in Christ? Do the participants view the eucharistic celebration as the culmination of their shared faith? Finally, how do these groups welcome those Catholics who have left the faith?

In asking these questions you may find equal benefit from having both an internal and external evaluation. Those who are very close to activities not undertaken with an evangelizing spirit may feel hurt if they perceive their efforts are not valued. An internal evaluation may be difficult for some to hear, but necessary. It may also allow those who run non-evangelizing ministries to revisit the reasons why the groups were formed originally. Such evaluations can help these ministries add elements that deepen each member's faith and love of Christ. It also may help change the mind-set of the parish and old ways of being Church, which may no longer speak to where people are at.

Having outsiders evaluate your programs also provides great value because it gives the community a chance to share their experiences and perceptions of evangelization. Leaving ourselves open to the critique of others can be painful. We like to hold on to what is comfortable. When we allow ourselves to be vulnerable and ask, "Why are we doing this?" substantial change can result.

When looking at the demographics of a parish we must assess whether and how each group is being trained to evangelize. How are we sharing the message of evangelization, and training others? Can parishioners articulate what evangelization is in one sentence? How do we reach out to individuals who fall within the parish boundaries but don't attend Mass? The task will be to develop a strategy for each group. Start small and be faithful with the follow-up. Affirm the places where evangelization is taking root and encourage growth where it is not. Don't spend time kicking down doors that aren't open, but where there is an open door, enter in.

Another important step is deciding what portion of the parish budget will go toward reaching out to lapsed Catholics and the unchurched. Most parishes spend the majority of their budget on religious education for children. But the question must be raised: Has it worked? Should we feel guilty for even broaching the topic?

Let's be honest: We have a generation of young adults who have expert skills at making cloth banners and coloring "God Loves Me" posters, yet who have no idea who Jesus is or what the basic tenets of the faith are. Are we bold enough to look at other models of teaching our children that involve parents as the primary educators? When the parents are not growing in faith, faith is negligible in their children. When parents are involved in Church and are growing in their faith, they make sure the children follow their lead.

When considering how the parish reaches out to those who are lapsed in the faith, we should ensure that there are events and initiatives designed for those who don't believe or who are apathetic about religion. Do we invite others who have left to come and take another look? What are our avenues of communication with those who no longer attend Mass? Do we think that we could attract people by advertising in a parish bulletin or the diocesan newspaper? How would a lapsed Catholic respond to an advertisement that has an icon of Jesus or a saint, a Scripture verse, or something written in Latin? We would do well to learn some techniques from Hollywood and Madison Avenue in this regard.

Is our message filled with "churchy" language familiar to faithful Catholics but confusing to non-believers? This is where collaboration with those in your target audience is vital. Perhaps the young adults in your parish can design and run the outreach programs to other young adults. If your target is outreach ministry to business professionals, have other professionals review the material first. Spiritual advice from a pastor or bishop may not attract a successful person in the business sector. However, they likely will respond more favorably to words spoken by a successful colleague in their field who understands the pressures and commitments of life in corporate America. Identify the business leaders, lawyers, doctors, nurses, professors, athletes, or leaders in other fields who would attract people to hear about the convergence of faith and work.

In planning new initiatives for those who have drifted away from the Church we should be clear about our objectives in order to evaluate their effectiveness. The number of people who attend a particular outreach event should not necessarily be the benchmark because we know that the Gospel is spread through relationships, one person at a time. If one person shows up and they were in some way touched by God's grace, then the event was a success.

If you decide to have a listening session for those who have left the Church then the objective may include providing a safe, non-judgmental environment in which people can speak, vent, or explain why they left. I'm sure every practicing Catholic knows of at least one Catholic who no longer worships on Sunday that they could invite. In evaluating the session, we can ask if we encouraged each participant to bring a friend. Was the lead time appropriate? Was there an atmosphere of hospitality? Did people who came to vent leave feeling welcomed, respected, and listened to? Did we truly listen rather than try to defend the Church or the poor behavior of others? Did we offer follow-up opportunities to those who may have theological issues with the faith so the dialogue can be continued? These are just a few ways to evaluate new programs.

The Role of the Parish Staff in Modeling a Missionary Character
In the diocese of Paterson, New Jersey, the bishop has mandated that every parish have an evangelization director who should form a team of faith-filled parishioners to help the parish fulfill its mission of evangelization. "The parish evangelization director must be a permanent member of all staff and parish council meetings. In this way, evangelization can remain a fundamental dimension of all parish ministries. Since the mandate to evangelize is from the Lord himself, we must say with St. Paul, 'Woe to me if I do not preach the Gospel'" (see 1 Corinthians 9:16).[70]

The parish evangelization director assists the pastor in ensuring that evangelization guides all that we do as the body of Christ. A parish may decide to have monthly formation meetings to help teach about evangelization, learn tools for reaching out beyond the community, and provide opportunities to encourage and learn from each other. There is a synergy that exists when groups meet and renewed energy is given to evangelization. Again, it is not the responsibility of one person, but an evangelization director and core group of people can ensure that evangelization is a common thread to all that we do as Church.

I was at a meeting once where those in attendance were sincere in their desire to form more community within the parish—a noble idea. The conversation there centered on having donuts and bagels after Mass and holding hands during the Our Father. As I was sitting there I was thinking, what brings a sports team together? What brings political parties together? What brings an army or a team of doctors or science researchers together? Holding hands before a meeting? Donuts? I don't think so. What brings them together is a common goal, and there is no more worthy goal for a parish than to bring a person into a vibrant relationship with the living God. This goal hasn't changed in two thousand years: It is why Christ formed the Church.

This focus should permeate all we do as members of the Church, and especially as a parish staff. The staff is invaluable as they often provide the first contact with people who are seeking a way back to the Church. Their welcome, their smile, their patience, their prompt follow-up, their care, their concern, and their understanding must model Christ to those who call, e-mail, and enter through the door. We must view every person as the lost sheep. We never know who God will bring through the door, and an untrained, antagonistic, hostile staff person is detrimental to the mission of evangelization.

These are a few ways that we can begin to change a culture which has traditionally been passive toward evangelization. Holy Mother Church is calling us to be active.

Mary, Star of the New Evangelization
Much has been written about the one who says so little in the Gospels, Mary, star of the New Evangelization. Her few brief words

and actions recorded in the New Testament draw Christians to contemplate her humility, her gift of motherhood, and her role in salvation history. While there is one mediator between God and man, Jesus Christ,[71] our union with Jesus allows us to share in the work of evangelization and participate in the saving work of Christ through the Church. No one has participated more beautifully in this effort than Mary. Her total surrender to God brought forth the savior to the world.

In concluding this book I would like to focus on a few short verses from Luke's Gospel. These verses draw our attention to Mary as the model of evangelization through her receptive listening and active response to the Word of God.

> The angel said to her, "The Holy Spirit will come upon you, and the power of the Most High will overshadow you; therefore the child to be born will be holy; he will be called Son of God. And now, your relative Elizabeth in her old age has also conceived a son; and this is the sixth month for her who was said to be barren. For nothing will be impossible with God." Then Mary said, "Here am I, the servant of the Lord; let it be with me according to your word." Then the angel departed from her. (Luke 1:35–38)

The Annunciation reveals the triune nature of God as Father, Son, and Holy Spirit, for they are present in the response given to Mary when she asks: "How can this be?" (Luke 1:34). Through accepting the divine invitation, Mary put God's plan of redemption into motion. Her "fiat" brought forward the New Adam through a New Eve and inaugurated the New Covenant in the person of Jesus Christ. Her passivity in hearing the Word of the Lord is now acted upon. With full consent of her will, in freedom, Mary speaks: "Let it be with me according to your word." This external response is a reflection of her interior disposition, one that is fully given over to God.

Dianne Traflet writes beautifully about this interior renewal as it relates to Mary and her influence on St. Edith Stein in her book *Saint Edith Stein: A Spiritual Portrait,* and provides some insight into Mary's motherhood. "This 'renewal of true interior life' is the key to fulfilling a vocation of Christian leadership. Mary could lead because she could follow. She could be fruitful because she was always empty of self. She could give her 'yes' to motherhood because she first had given her 'yes' to childhood, that is, her assent to handmaiden. Her ability to recognize herself as a handmaiden indicates her childlike humility and her mature readiness to become a mother. Her spiritual childhood necessarily preceded her motherhood."

The principal agent in evangelization is the Holy Spirit. In placing herself at the disposition of the Lord, Mary becomes a handmaid, full of the Holy Spirit, full of grace. Mary's first response to the Spirit after her consent is to go "with haste to a Judean town in the hill country" to tell the good news to her relatives. The word used for *haste* in Greek is σπουδή, which better signifies *eagerness*.[72]

Mary, now pregnant with Jesus, sets out to evangelize with eagerness, to bring this good news to others beginning with her family. Mary brings the Word of God, incarnate within her, to the house of Zechariah as she greets Elizabeth. It is important to note that the initial proclamation takes place not in the temple nor in a synagogue but in a home. This proclamation is what we have come to call the Magnificat and comes from the lips of Mary when she says that her soul "magnifies" the Lord. Mary now becomes the master catechist as she recalls God's marvelous acts of faithfulness, mercy, and blessings.

Mary accepted the Word of God revealed to her at the Annunciation and remained faithful to that Word throughout her life, even unto the cross. Mary "stands out among the poor and humble of the Lord, who confidently hope for and receive salvation from Him."[73] After a long period of waiting the times are fulfilled in her, the exalted Daughter of Sion, and the new plan of salvation is established."

The Church, too, becomes a mother through accepting with fidelity the Word of God. This maternal characteristic of the Church was expressed in a particularly eloquent way by the apostle Paul when he wrote: "My little children, for whom I am again in the pain of childbirth until Christ is formed in you" (Galatians 4:19).

Yes, Mary is truly the star of the New Evangelization. Those who seek her, flee to her protection, implore her help, and seek her intercession know of her maternal love, for they are never left unaided. The task that lies ahead for the Catholic Church is not daunting or overwhelming, for we have a mother who goes before us, who calls us to discipleship. She was there when Herod threatened Jesus's life, she was present at Cana, she stood faithfully at the cross and gathered with the apostles in prayer at Pentecost. May we never lower our heads in despair, never become overwhelmed and lose hope, for Mary has lead the way and now reigns in heaven.

In embracing the word of God and announcing it to a world that so desperately needs to hear it, we too can bring others to what the world cannot give: Jesus Christ, the Prince of Peace.

NOTES

1. *Evangelii Nuntiandi*, 14.
2. *Redemptoris Missio*, 33.
3. *Redemptoris Missio*, 3.
4. Pope Benedict XVI, Greeting to Students of the Roman Pontifical Universities, St. Peter's Square (October, 2007). Available at www.archsa.org/evangelization/documents/evangelize2.ppt.
5. *CARA Report*, Summer 2012. Quoted at http://nineteensixty-four.blogspot.com/2012/05/microscoping-view-of-us-catholic.html.
6. Quoted at http://www.doctorsofthecatholicchurch.com/J.html.
7. *CCC*, 133, quoting *Dei Verbum*, 25; referencing Philippians 3:8 and St. Jerome, *Commentariorum in Isaiam libri xviii* prologue: PL 24, 17b.
8. Catherine of Siena, quoted in Thomas McDermott, o.p., "Catherine of Siena's Teaching on Self-Knowledge," *New Blackfriars*, November 2007, pp. 637ff.
9. Quoted at http://en.radiovaticana.va/articolo.asp?c=528388.
10. *Dei Verbum*, 2, referencing Ephesians 1:9; 2:18; 2 Peter 1:4. Available at http://www.vatican.va/archive/hist_councils/ii_vatican_council/documents/vat-ii_const_19651118_dei-verbum_en.html.
11. The Court of the Gentiles referred to an area on the Temple Mount in Jerusalem where non-Jews could enter and ask religious questions.
12. *Verbum Domini*, 91. Available at http://www.vatican.va/holy_father/benedict_xvi/apost_exhortations/documents/hf_ben-xvi_exh_20100930_verbum-domini_en.html.
13. The practice of giving a percentage of your income to the poor in Judaism is called *tzedaka*. Deuteronomy 19:9–10 speaks of generosity towards your poor brother and Leviticus 19:9–10 calls those who harvest a field to leave the edges unharvested for the widow and orphan and to not harvest a second time—leave the grapes that have fallen for the "poor and alien."
14. *Deus Caritas Est*, 22. Available at http://www.vatican.va/holy_father/benedict_xvi/encyclicals/documents/hf_ben-xvi_enc_20051225_deus-caritas-est_en.html.
15. *Evangelii Nuntiandi*, 41. Quoted at http://www.op.org/sites/www.op.org/files/public/documents/fichier/byrne1989_minpreaching_en.pdf.
16. Pope Benedict's message for the 83rd World Mission Sunday, quoting *Evangelii Nuntiandi*, 1.

17. Adapted from St. Thomas Aquinas, *Aquinas Scripture Series: Commentary on the Gospel of John, Chapters 1–5,* Weisheipl and Larcher, trans. (Washington, D.C.: Catholic University of America Press, 2010), p. 211.

18. St. Augustine, *Confessions,* Book 1, Chapter 1.

19. Quoted at http://monicameuse.blogspot.com/2011/11/if-you-cant-feed-one-thousand-people.html.

20. Jean Vanier, *Becoming Human* (Toronto: House of Anansi, 2008), p 163.

21. Quoted in Peter Kreeft, *Back to Virtue* (San Francisco: Ignatius, 1986), p. 146.

22. *Mishnah,* Yebamot 16: 3a–e.

23. Pope Benedict XVI, *On the Way to Jesus Christ,* (San Francisco: Ignatius, 2005), pp. 48–50.

24. *Dignitatis Humanae,* 11.

25. National Church Life Survey Research, Occasional Paper 13:2009.

26. Archbishop Rino Fisichella, *Jesus "Proclaimer of the Gospel."* Available at http://www.vatican.va/jubilee_2000/magazine/documents/ju_mag_dec-1996_fisichella_en.html.

27. Fisichella, *Jesus "Proclaimer of the Gospel."*

28. Quoted in Shane Claiborne, *The Irresistible Revolution: Living as an Ordinary Radical* (Grand Rapids: Zondervan, 2008).

29. The magisterium is the teaching authority of the Catholic Church, the bishops in union with the pope (see *CCC,* 100).

30. Romans 16:17; 1 Corinthians 1:10–12; Galatians 3:1–3.

31. St. Catherine of Siena, *Dialogue,* 1.

32. Quoted at http://www.catholicworker.org/dorothyday/ddbiographytext.cfm?Number=71.

33. Arthur J. Serratelli, *Evangelization: Grace and Vocation,* 30. Available at http://www.patersondiocese.org/pdf/en_pastoral_evangelization.pdf.

34. Kenneth E. Bailey, *Poet and Peasant and Through Peasant Eyes,* (Grand Rapids, Eerdmans, 1994) p. 48.

35. *The New Evangelization for the Transmission of the Christian Faith (Lineamenta),* 31.

36. Quoted at http://peacetraditions.wordpress.com/people/.

37. *The New Evangelization for the Transmission of the Christian Faith (Lineamenta),* preface.

38. Quoted at http://catholic-quote.blogspot.com/2010/12/st-maximilian-kolbe.html.

39. St. Jerome. See also *CCC,* 1340–1344.

40. *Ecclesia de Eucharistia,* 22.

41. John Paul II, encyclical *Ecclesia de Eucharistia,* 60.

42. Quoted in Peter C. Phan, ed., *The Gift of the Church: A Textbook on Ecclesiology in Honor of Patrick Granfield* (Collegeville, Minn.: Michael Glazier, 2000), p. 188.

43. Quoted in Sharon Senna, *Wisdom: Things I Wish I Knew at Twenty-Two* (Tucson, Ariz.: Wheatmark, 2010), p. 72.

44. Pope Benedict XVI, Address at the 46th World Communications Day.

45. Pope Benedict XVI, *Salt of the Earth: Christianity and the Catholic Church at the End of the Millennium—An Interview With Peter Seewald* (San Francisco: Ignatius, 1997), p. 117.

46. *Dei Verbum,* 9.

47. In Greek the word used is *splanchnizomai* translated as "pity" or "compassion." It is the same word used in the story of the Good Samaritan, Luke 10:30. The root of the word, *splachnon,* refers to the inner organs and is used to refer to inner yearnings and the heart which is the seat of feelings in antiquity.

48. See also Matthew 14:14; 15:32; 20:34.

49. *Illustrated London News,* November 24, 1934. Quoted in *The Collected Works of G.K. Chesterton, Vol. 36: The Illustrated London News* (San Francisco: Ignatius, 2011).

50. Pope Benedict XVI, "Find New Ways to Announce Christ," Zenit, February 8, 2008. Available at http://www.zenit.org/article-21720?l=english.

51. Pope Benedict XVI, 40th Anniversary of Vatican II's "Ad Gentes," March 13, 2006.

52. *Ad Gentes,* 2.

53. The word *home* is used thirty times in the Gospels and the word *house* is used ninety-nine times. So much of Jesus's healing, teaching, forgiving and sharing meals takes place in the home. For more insight see *Jesus in the House: Gospel Reflections on Christ's Presence in the Home* by Franciscan Media.

54. *Evangelii Nuntiandi,* 17, 21, 48ff.

55. Pope Benedict XVI, 40th Anniversary of Vatican II's "Ad Gentes," March 13, 2006.

56. *God's Valiant Warrior,* by Dennis Berry, S.T. (Philadelphia: Missionary Cenacle, 1994), p. 179.

57. *Code of Canon Law,* 528.1.

58. Fulton Sheen, quoted in *Radio Replies* Volume 1, (St. Paul, Minn.: Radio Replies Press Society, 1938), p. ix.

59. The Council of Rome, held in 382 AD under the authority of Pope Damasus, gave a complete list of canonical books of the Old and New Testaments.

60. *CCC,* 780.

61. Quoted at http://www.essene.com/B%27nai-Amen/j-saying.htm.

62. St. Augustine, *City of God* 19, 13,1.

63. *Gaudium et Spes,* 4.

64. *The New Evangelization for the Transmission of the Christian Faith (Lineamenta),* 10, available at http://www.vatican.va/roman_curia/synod/documents/rc_synod_doc_20110202_lineamenta-xiii-assembly_en.html.

65. *The New Evangelization for the Transmission of the Christian Faith (Lineamenta),* 10.

66. St. Francis de Sales, *Introduction to the Devout Life,* Part 3, Chapter 35.

67. Baptism is the foundation of communion among all Christians: *CCC,* 1271.

68. Available at http://www.vatican.va/holy_father/benedict_xvi/apost_letters/documents/hf_ben-xvi_apl_20100921_ubicumque-et-semper_en.html.

69. See Acts 2:42.

70. Arthur J. Serratelli, *Evangelization: Grace and Vocation,* 72. Available at http://www.patersondiocese.org/pdf/en_pastoral_evangelization.pdf.

71. See 1 Timothy 2:5.

72. Balz and Schneider, *Exegetical Dictionary of the New Testament,* vol. 3 (Grand Rapids: Eerdmans), p. 267.

73. *Lumen Gentium,* 55.

There is a leader's guide available for this book, which highlights ways *Jesus the Evangelist: A Gospel Guide to the New Evangelization* can be used with parish leaders and with small groups. This brief overview gives helpful tips and guidelines to enhance the use of this book in making your parish a more evangelizing faith community. Go to www.AmericanCatholic/guide to download this free resource.